RUNNING FROM
COVID
IN OUR
RV COCOON

GERRI ALMAND

BROWN POSEY PRESS

an imprint of Sunbury Press, Inc.
Mechanicsburg, PA USA

an imprint of Sunbury Press, Inc.
Mechanicsburg, PA USA

For information about special discounts for bulk purchases, please contact Sunbury Press Orders Dept. at (855) 338-8359 or orders@sunburypress.com.

To request one of our authors for speaking engagements or book signings, please contact Sunbury Press Publicity Dept. at publicity@sunburypress.com.

FIRST BROWN POSEY PRESS EDITION: May 2021

Set in Adobe Garamond | Interior design by Crystal Devine | Cover design by Terry Kennedy | Edited by Abigail Henson.

Publisher's Cataloging-in-Publication Data
Names: Almand, Gerri, author.
Title: Running from covid in our rv cocoon / Gerri Almand.
Description: First trade paperback edition. | Mechanicsburg, PA : Brown Posey Press, 2021.
Summary: As the coronavirus pandemic erupts, two grizzled old geezers leave in their RV on a humorous, paradoxical journey of both losing and finding freedom.
Identifiers: ISBN : 978-1-62006-525-9 (softcover).
Subjects: SPORTS & RECREATION / Camping | TRAVEL / Special Interest / Family | TRAVEL / Special Interest / Senior | TRAVEL / Essays & Travelogues | HUMOR / Topic / Travel | TRAVEL / United States / General.

Product of the United States of America
0 1 1 2 3 5 8 13 21 34 55

Continue the Enlightenment!

THIS BOOK IS DEDICATED TO
the many wonderful fulltime RVers we've met
during the past year who have helped us transition
into this unfettered and untethered lifestyle.

CONTENTS

ACKNOWLEDGMENTS

The members of my Florida Writers Association critique group have shown great patience in reading multiple chapters of this manuscript. I appreciate their astute yet gentle recommendations and unwavering support. These ladies now know more about both me and RVing than they ever wanted to know. Hugs and thanks to Susan Breakiron-Lowe, Arleen Mariotti, E.M. St. Pierre, Eileen Hector, and Gail Dudley.

Three RVing Beta readers read and offered comments on this manuscript. Nadyne Huber, Cindy Lougheed, and Liza Simpson—I so appreciate your feedback. Steak dinners will be coming your way down the road when we next meet in person.

I thank the friends who gave permission for me to use their names and their stories in this work. To Jack and Nadyne Huber, Denise Ordonio, Les and Kerry Jones, Steve and Sandra Vigil, Craig and Arline Bringhurst, Bill and Diane Wolff, and Chris Wickland and Liza Simpson—I hope our paths will continue to cross on the highways across America.

Finally, my husband, Michael Hamlin, and my daughter Kate . . . you give my life shape and meaning. And yes, Michael, maybe I do need to finally say 'thank you' for bringing an RV into my life.

Dialogue in this book came from my memory. I have tried to remain true to the content although the actual words might have differed.

CHAPTER I

A NOMAD STATE OF MIND

Were the eleven pairs of shoes a premonition of what lay ahead? When my husband Michael and I packed for a two-month RV road trip in early February 2020, I had no way of knowing my life was about to change in both devastating and glorious ways. That I'd never go home again, and that not only would it be okay, but it'd also be the best thing that ever happened to me.

We'd just upgraded to a larger motorhome, moving from a 26-ft. Class C Thor Four Winds to a 33-ft. Class A Thor ACE. I celebrated the spaciousness of our new digs. The 6-ft. closet in the bedroom filled me with joy every time I opened one of its doors. I had a place to hang clothes, drawers to stuff with socks and underwear, and enough cabinets to stash almost anything else I chose to bring. Like eleven pairs of shoes.

I counted the shoes again to make sure I hadn't made a mistake. Then I threw in another pair, just for fun.

Michael and I had vacillated several times on whether to become full-time nomads. During our four years of RVing, we'd camped in forty-nine states and put 50,000 miles on the odometer. Michael had lobbied hard to go full-time, and I'd finally agreed a couple of years earlier. However, medical issues popped up, and we had to delay our plan to hit the road. Now, neither of us was quite as sound and hardy as we'd been four years earlier when we'd first started RVing. At our ages, the thought of selling our comfortable, paid-for home in Tampa, Florida, seemed irresponsible.

"We can't RV forever," I'd argued. "What happens when one of us gets sick?"

"We'll deal with it when it happens, if it ever does," Michael said. "We'll travel as long as we can, and we'll figure out where we want to live when we can't. Then we'll buy a condo or rent an apartment and settle down."

"But if one of us gets sick, don't you think it'd be nice to have friends visit us in the hospital? Would you really want to be in Santa Fe, or Portland, or somewhere on the West Coast where no one knows us?"

"We'll make new friends," my persuasive husband had said. "We'll worry about all that when the time comes. Right now, there's no reason not to go."

I had finally resolved my reluctance to RV travel and had embraced the notion of full-time nomadism. I'd already started paring down my possessions and discovered I loved the freedom of minimalism. It felt good to travel light, to have everything I needed within arm's reach in our RV. (I refused to consider that twelve pairs of shoes may have been a few too many.) I'd given up gardening for writing, and I could easily write in my new 'RV office,' regardless of where I happened to be. Plus, travel gave me more new writing material than I'd ever be able to process. Our new RV felt like it could be my home.

When we left Tampa in mid-February, we never imagined our RV trip would be so life-altering. We'd heard that scientists had identified a new and dangerous virus in China, but China was far away. We didn't give it a second thought. It was not something for us to even consider.

Need I foreshadow the rest of this story with the famous Robert Burns' line that "The best laid schemes of mice and men Go oft awry?"

"Crazy to be leaving Florida in the winter, don't you think? Hope we're not going to regret this," I said to Michael as we loaded our new rig for a two-month maiden voyage.

"We should be okay. We're staying far enough south we shouldn't run into any snow."

After this two-month road trip, we planned to return to Tampa, sell our house, and leave Florida again by June, this time as full-time RVers. I was excited.

Our first stop of the trip was a Spirit of the Road RV Rally in Live Oak, Florida. Two non-profit, online RV communities—the Escapees and RVillage—sponsored the event. Both groups had thousands of members, impressive websites, Facebook pages, magazines and newsletters, and multiple benefits and discount services for their members. Many of the members lived full-time on the road. We figured this would be a great place to learn more about full-time RVing.

The venue for the rally was perfect. The Spirit of the Suwannee Music Park Campground boasted six-hundred sites and over eighty acres for primitive camping and boondocking. Designed as a concert venue, the facility had both inside and outside stages, a coffee shop that transformed into a banquet hall for dining and dancing during evening concerts, and huge open areas for lawn seating, vendor tents, and food trucks.

In one of the large open fields, rally organizers had erected five Firebirds—huge, hollow metal frames with cutout designs. At night, volunteers filled the structures with firewood, which they'd light when the sun went down. The open fires heated the metal and created beautiful colors and designs through the openings. These Firebirds also provided much-appreciated heat during the outdoor nightly concerts. RVers squeezed their folding chairs as close as possible to the twenty-foot structures. Few seemed to notice or care that their hair and coats became covered with white ashes.

By the end of the first evening, the friendly, relaxed atmosphere had awed and enchanted us. We heard there were almost two thousand RVers at the rally, running the gamut from newbies to decades-long full-timers.

Despite our new equipment, Michael and I thought of ourselves as experienced. We'd driven many miles across many states. We'd soon learn we were neophytes when it came to living on the road.

〔⊓ᴥ〕

Despite all the miles we'd covered and the time we'd spent on the road, I still felt I was missing a fundamental understanding of the 'why' of RVing. Surely there must be an underlying philosophy to explain why so many folks had taken up this lifestyle. During the past four years, the gypsies we'd met during the past four years never mentioned Henry David Thoreau or minimalism, which were the philosophical underpinnings of my current RV formulations. Nor did these full-timers have missions of hitting all the major tourist spots or putting stickers on the United States and Canadian sticker maps. Rarely did we hear RVers talk about major attractions, except for occasional rallies, RV shows, or national parks. They almost seemed to be moving for the pure joy of moving, like an aimless and pointless wandering from one stop to the next.

I had concluded earlier that an 'RV lifestyle' didn't exist, that there were as many motivations and approaches to RV travel as there were RVers. Still, the pull to live as nomads seemed too widespread to dismiss quite so easily. There had to be a common denominator somewhere, even if it was unconscious.

The keynote speaker at the rally was the nomadic RV icon, Bob Wells. I could hardly wait to hear him speak. I had a niggling sense he might give me answers, and if not answers, at least new ideas to consider.

I was right. The larger-than-life RV superstar, with his bushy white hair and beard, took the stage in the Main Hall to a standing-room-only audience of hundreds of RVers. Some had heard Bob Wells before, but for many, this was the first time.

I found Bob Wells brilliant, articulate, and charismatic. Despite his off-the-grid van lifestyle for several decades, I thought Wells must have found time to join Toastmasters International or the National Speakers Association. He presented with such softly-spoken authority and with such conversational intimacy it felt like he was talking directly to me.

Wells began by saying he felt like he'd never fit in, had never been comfortable in his own skin while living in a regular house and working traditional jobs. He'd always felt something was not quite right. When a sticky divorce left him financially strapped to pay alimony, child support, and housing for his estranged family, he turned an old van into an apartment. Wells lived in Anchorage, Alaska, at the time of his divorce, where temperatures sometimes dropped to thirty degrees below zero during the winters. He reported running propane heaters twenty-four hours a day to keep from freezing to death. He joined a gym so he could shower every day. He said that he hated his life at first, then found it tolerable, and finally, he grew to "adore it."

Wells believed we were all programmed to be nomads, that it was in our DNA, and that it had originated with the hunters and gatherers who moved seasonally in search of food. After years of research in science, religion, and philosophy, Wells believed he had found an objective standard for how humans could best live. That standard was nomadism.

Wells viewed community as the heart of human relationships and had set up non-profit organizations to help RVers find community and live effectively as nomads. He maintained a popular website at www. CheapRVLiving.com. For a monthly membership fee, one could view hundreds of his YouTube videos and podcasts.

It took me a couple of hours to process the ideas Bob Wells had presented. Later in the afternoon, I said to Michael, "You know, if Henry David Thoreau were still alive, I think he'd choose to live in an RV rather than a cabin in the woods."

"What are you talking about? What made you say that?"

"It's all about simplicity, letting go of our attachments," I said. The synapses in my brain cells were firing in overdrive, and I felt like I'd burst out of my skin with excitement. "Remember what Bob Wells said about how modern society has it all wrong, that we love our things and use people when we should be loving people and using things?"

"What I remember most about his talk was the Carl Jung part, about how we have these archaic man prototypes buried in our psyches, sort of a primordial survivor instinct."

"Yeah, and from an anthropological point of view, the history of living in bands as hunters and gatherers, moving seasonally in search of animals to hunt and plants to eat . . ." I said, my voice loud with excitement. Based on his research, Wells believed a band of about 150 people was ideal for safety and community. I continued, "These hunters and gatherers couldn't collect things, not when they had to pick up and move every few months or so. Possessions become burdens."

These were the kinds of explanations I'd been looking for since Michael had talked me into us buying an RV and seeing the country. Now I had finally found a contemporary, twenty-first-century guru who had filled in the missing pieces to the puzzle better than I could ever have dreamed of doing on my own. Bob Wells became my new RV mentor and philosophical maharishi.

Wells believed RV rallies provided the settings for smaller tribes to come together to form larger communities. From those larger communities, people could meet to develop new, smaller, and more intimate groups and bands. I realized that Michael and I had stumbled upon a new way of viewing life in a tin can house on wheels.

"I feel like I'm finally pulling it all together," I said to Michael. "I'm seeing life in this RV in a different way. I believe I'm going to be happier as a nomad than I have anywhere else. I think I've found a nomad state of mind."

CHAPTER 2

FINDING COMMUNITY

"What happened to your leg?" someone asked David, pointing to a large bandage on one of his shins.

"I fell off my bicycle this morning," he said with a chuckle. "I'm not really supposed to be riding a bike since I can't turn my head and my balance is bad."

We had just met David and Denise Ordonio, a couple from Maryland whose rig was set up a short distance from ours. Our next-door neighbors, Jack and Nadyne Huber, were hosting a get-to-know-your-neighbor happy hour at their campsite. It was the second day of the RVillage Rally, and simultaneous happy hours were taking place all over the campground. Jack introduced himself and Nadyne as RVillage Emissaries,

"What's an RVillage Emissary?" I asked

"It's a representative for RVillage who hosts bi-weekly get-togethers for RVers to attend and get to know each other," Nadyne said.

Although we changed the topic of conversation, Nadyne and Jack had planted a seed in my mind. I remembered thinking Michael and I might enjoy doing something like that, maybe sometime in the future. We were happy they'd invited us. We liked these people and wanted to be a part of their tribe, as my new RV guru Bob Wells had described small groups of RVers who hung out together.

About a dozen folks had dropped by the Hubers' site, a perfect number to mingle and get to know each other. Michael and I knew no one initially, but as the beer and wine flowed, we felt we were making new best-friends-forever.

David was friendly and outgoing, by far the most vivacious one in the group. "I broke my neck, and now all the bones are fused," he said. "I now have to say 'yes' or 'no' with my whole body." He grinned as he bowed deeply up and down for 'yes' and twisted his entire torso back and forth for 'no.' He also said he'd had a history of strokes that forced him to retire early from federal government employment. David wouldn't tell his age, at times laughing that he was ninety-six, at other times merely saying he was probably a lot older than anyone would guess. I couldn't decide how old I thought he was.

Denise, a licensed massage therapist with strawberry blonde hair and freckles, was more reserved than her effervescent spouse. Denise later told me David had suffered his first stroke in March 2018, at which time she retired from work to care for him. Lying in a hospital bed, David had told her that he wanted to spend the rest of his life traveling in an RV if he recovered enough.

David made progress, and the couple began camping again in their teardrop camper. In September 2018, they upgraded their teardrop camper for a 31-ft. Class C Minnie Winnie. Longer trips started in June 2019. From observations and conversations, it seemed that Denise was somewhat of a caretaker for David and the one in charge of the RV. She did all the driving and most of all the physical work because of David's physical issues. We were surprised to learn they didn't tow a car.

I understood the bicycle part of the story, though, and why David had taken the risk of riding one. The campground was huge, and the main event areas were far away from most of the campsites. Still, considering someone with his physical impairments, it didn't seem a surprise he'd had an accident. The bandaged scrape on his knee looked painful.

When the happy hour ended, Denise invited us back to their rig for spaghetti, which she'd been simmering in a crockpot all afternoon. We brought a salad. Their RV reflected Denise's craft and carpentry skills. She'd built and inserted dividers and organizers in all the cabinets and drawers. She'd even figured out how to store her massage table in case she wanted to use it.

"I sure wish we were smart enough to figure out how to organize like this," I'd said.

When we got back to our rig, I said to Michael, "I wonder what they'd do if an emergency arose. That guy has all kinds of medical problems." Michael agreed it seemed somewhat risky.

The next morning, we learned first-hand what would happen if a medical emergency arose for an RVer without a car. While we were drinking coffee with David and Denise in the park café, Denise received a phone call from David's physician in Maryland. The doctor had received the lab report from blood work drawn the previous week. The results showed sky-high potassium levels. The doctor's office had tried to fax a prescription to the two small pharmacies in Live Oak, Florida, but neither drug store stocked the medication.

"Your doctor says you've got to go to the nearest Urgent Care," Denise said to David. "I'll see what I can find."

There wasn't much to find. Live Oak was a small, poor, rural town in the northern part of Florida bordering the Georgia State line, about sixty miles west of Jacksonville and ninety miles east of Tallahassee.

Denise returned to our café table a few minutes later. "I can't believe this. Live Oak lists two Urgent Cares, but one of them has disconnected their phone, and the other one doesn't answer. What the hell?"

"Try Lake City," I said. "It's a bit bigger." I knew this part of North Florida well, having grown up in nearby Madison County.

A couple of minutes later, Denise returned. "I found one, and the woman said they're not very busy." Turning to her husband, she said, "Your doctor's office is faxing your records right now."

"We'll take you," I said. The offer was spontaneous. According to Denise, David's potassium levels were high enough to trigger a heart attack.

"Okay. Thanks," Denise said.

We flagged our waitress for our checks. Michael had arranged for RV service in the afternoon, so I'd be driving Denise and David while he tended to our rig. I made a quick google search on my cell phone. The clinic was almost thirty miles away. We scurried back to our rigs to get ready, and I picked up my passengers ten minutes later.

I felt anxious, tense. The responsibility of getting a dangerously ill man for medical care before an emergency happened felt like a boulder on my chest. I gripped the steering wheel and turned on to Interstate 10, heading west. We'd have to go at least twenty miles on the highway before turning south on a county road to Lake City. I vowed not to speed, despite my sense of urgency over our mission.

In the backseat, David maintained a steady stream of talk while Denise sat quietly in the front passenger seat. "How are you feeling?" I asked him, unable to shake my fear that he would keel over.

"Oh, I'm good. Don't feel any different than usual." After several attempts at back-and-forth conversation, I gave up. His voice was too soft for me to hear over the road noise. My stress level mounted by the moment. I knew I needed to calm down.

"Tell me again what the doctor said." This time David directed his comment to Denise. She started repeating the info about the high potassium levels.

Suddenly, an alert popped up on my car's dash.

"Uh-oh," I interrupted. "We might have a problem. My low tire pressure warning just came on."

"Those things never work right," Denise said. "We'll be okay."

Her reaction surprised me. "This alert has never been wrong," I said. "I've had a couple of tire leaks before."

"Everything feels okay," Denise said. "Nothing seems to be pulling."

I didn't answer. I gripped the steering wheel a bit tighter and slowed down to about sixty. Cars and semis whizzed past as if my car stood still. We were driving on a long, rural stretch of Interstate 10, with exits ten to fifteen miles apart. If the tire went flat, we'd sit for hours before roadside assistance showed up. Plus, there was a significant piece of information about my C-Max that my two passengers, one with a potential medical crisis, did not know. This car did not have a spare, and in the event of a blowout, I'd have to call a tow truck and have it flat-bed hauled to a tire shop. It'd happened before. Twice. I silently cursed myself again for having bought a car with such a pain-in-the-ass, stupid-beyond-words, no-spare-tire design. (Other than not having a spare, I adored my little hybrid.)

I drove another couple of minutes in silence, filled with anxiety and dread. Seeing a sign for a rest area ahead, I said, "I'm going to pull over and at least take a look."

We pulled in, parked, and the three of us walked around the car a couple of times. I found it hard to imagine, watching David, that this was a medical emergency. He acted so chipper and energetic. Denise's solemn demeanor told a different story, however. Her face and body language suggested stress and tension.

"They all look okay to me," Denise said.

"Yeah, we're fine," David said. "Let's keep going. I think your tire monitor has malfunctioned."

The damned tire monitor had not malfunctioned. One of these friggin' tires had a leak that could blow, and one of my passengers had a heart that could stop beating. The potential ramifications of whatever decision I made terrified me. Do we go, or do we stay?

I made a split-second calculation in my head and decided to defer to my passengers. They were the ones with the medical crisis. If something happened with either the car or with David, I might not feel quite as bad if they had made the decision. I shrugged and said, "Okay, we'll keep going."

We pulled back on the highway, and I slowed down to a cruise-controlled 55 mph speed, my teeth clenched and my breathing shallow. Why did I feel so responsible? No one could blame me for picking up a nail or something in a tire. My mechanic back home had checked the entire car, including the tires, five days earlier to make sure everything was good.

Denise had programmed the Urgent Care on Google Maps on her phone. I refrained from repeatedly asking her during the next twenty-one miles how far we had to go. The low tire pressure monitor didn't waver its alert. I thanked God it didn't beep or flash. My backseat passenger maintained a cheerful monologue as my anxiety rose by the minute and by the mile. How long did it take a punctured tire to deflate and for the rim to ride on the asphalt?

Denise googled tire stores as we neared the clinic and found one eight-tenths of a mile away. I drove to the front door, let my passengers out, and rushed to Discount Tire in Lake City. Whew!

The mechanic checked the pressure on all four tires. Three of my tires were at the recommended 36 psi. The back rear, however, was at only 25 psi. The guy patched the tire in less than an hour. He showed me a sliver of metal about an inch wide that had worked its way through the tread and triggered the leak.

I arrived back at the Urgent Care before David had even left the examining room. His affect was as bright as ever. We waited for almost an hour for his prescription, munching on locally grown fresh pecans to ease the hunger pangs in our stomachs. The drugstore owner must have owned a pecan grove. A huge stack of one-pound cellophane bags of the nuts, labeled 'Big Nuts' and the pharmacy logo, sat at the register. We'd all missed lunch for this emergency outing but didn't dare leave without David's medication.

I drove us back to the campground with relief and gratitude. I later realized I'd dodged a major bullet in a potentially dangerous area, that of towing a vehicle behind an RV.

If I'd not taken Denise and David to the Urgent Care in Lake City, I wouldn't have driven the car again until we hooked it to the rig and left the campground a couple of days later. I shuddered to imagine what would've happened if a tire had blown on the C-Max while we were tow-ing it behind the RV. We couldn't see our tow vehicle and would've been unaware of the problem. Just the day before, we'd attended an RV safe driving class during which the instructor warned that sparks triggered by a rim on asphalt could cause a toad to burst into flames. The fire could move through the electrical connections and enter the coach. My Good Samaritan deed had possibly paid off for Michael and me more than we would ever really know. It may have even saved our lives.

Denise dropped by the next day. "Just wanted to say thanks again and to give you these." She handed me a couple of hand-painted tile coasters wrapped with a ribbon.

"Is David okay? I've been really worried about him."

"Oh, he's fine. He started the new medication last night. We'll get his potassium levels checked again when we get to our next stop."

"That must have been terrifying for you, having his blood values so unstable that doctors sent you rushing to an Urgent Care clinic."

Denise shrugged. "You don't understand. A heart attack from high potassium is pretty far down on the list of things I worry about. There are many things, far worse than a heart attack, that could go wrong with David's body."

"Hugs," I said, reaching out to her. "You are a very brave and strong woman."

Denise's words would haunt me. I could only imagine the anxieties she lived with daily. Or the challenges she might face in the future with medical emergencies and decisions.

I found inspiration in the words Denise later shared with me. From the time of David's first stroke in 2018, the two of them had been inseparable. David had wanted to travel, and they'd made it happen. According to Denise, her husband was in his element during those four months of full-time RVing. "He thrived on the road, made friends everywhere we went. We never, ever second-guessed our decision. He was just so happy to be living his dream."

As Michael and I hit Interstate 10 heading west towards New Orleans, I thought about the dual alarms I'd just had—heart attacks and tire blowouts. Weren't we all, in various ways, playing Russian Roulette? Just because we didn't know what was going on inside our bodies didn't mean we didn't have timebombs ticking away, waiting to bring disaster. David and Denise were doing it right, following dreams while they still could. And now, Michael and I were on the way to doing the same. A few more months, and we'd be on the road full-time, too.

"Hey," I said to Michael. "Maybe we can hook up with David and Denise somewhere down the road."

"Sure, we're all Facebook friends now. It'll be easy to stay in touch."

That meet-up down the road with the Ordonios never happened. David had another stroke on March 24th, just six weeks after the RVillage Rally ended, and passed away five days later. It saddened us beyond words.

We'd not heard mainstream news reports for almost a week due to a combination of limited internet services and the rally keeping us busy. We'd heard, but forgotten, that China had reported an outbreak of a new unidentified and unnamed virus just before we left Tampa. We had no clue at the time that China's little virus might impact our lives.

This RV rally had been an eye-opener. The event had focused on creating community, and we'd drunk deeply of the Kool-Aid. We'd joined two RV clubs (the Escapees and RVillage), which would give us both online and in-person communities and resources in the future. We'd made friends with three new couples—Jack and Nadyne Huber, David and Denise Ordonio, and Les and Kerry Jones. Les and Kerry had camped on the side of our RV opposite the Hubers. While we'd not gotten to know them as well as we had the Hubers or the Ordonios, we would reconnect in-person with Les and Kerry less than three months down the road. We would stay in touch with all three couples on Facebook, and we would become very close friends with the Hubers, enjoying Zoom happy hours with them a couple of times each month.

My thoughts went deeper. As I thought back to the people we'd met at the rally, I realized David and Denise's mission was possibly universal among this gathering. Attendees were primarily older, retired people, and almost every one of us wore the wounds and scars of our wearied and losing battles with getting old. We all seemed to be out in the world searching for something. Was there a common denominator that drew this group of folks to the open road in their campers while other folks stayed put in their bricks-and-sticks houses?

I now believed I'd find community among RVers. David and Denise, Jack and Nadyne, and Les and Kerry were just the beginning.

The words of my favorite sixties' blues singer, Janis Joplin, came to mind, and I suddenly felt euphoric to be bouncing along this highway in my tin can house, my best friend at my side, the open road and unknown out the front windshield. Janis was right, and just like David and Denise, Michael and I were now off to get as much as we possibly could.

CHAPTER 3

BEADS ON BOURBON STREET

"Wow, what a rush that was," I said to Michael. "I'm just bubbling over with excitement about going full-time. Can you believe it?" We'd just left the RVillage rally and were heading towards New Orleans for Mardi Gras. In my typical state of impatience, I could hardly wait to get through this next leg of our trip, a necessary step towards our ultimate goal of making the road our home.

"Yeah, but we've got a lot of work waiting for us when we get back home, emptying and selling the house. I still think we should've planned just to keep going."

"I want to empty the house myself, and you wouldn't consider delaying the trip. You were hell-bent on testing out this new rig," I said. "I guess we'll get it all done when we get back, and then we'll be on the road for good."

We both had apprehensions about going to Mardi Gras. First, eight days seemed like an inordinate amount of time to spend drinking, partying, and watching parades. Secondly, we'd signed up with an RV tour company, which meant we'd be moving in a group every time we left the park. The caravan company had rented sites at the Bayou Segnette State Park in Westwego, Louisiana, seven miles south of downtown. Every morning we'd board a bus with about thirty other RVers and ride the thirty minutes into town. The driver would drop us off to watch parades, wander the streets, or whatever else we wanted to do. For us, it'd probably be squeezing into Bourbon Street bars to drink and listen to live music.

We'd taken a couple of trips before with this tour company. After the second trip, sixty-three days to and from Alaska in 2017, we'd sworn we'd never, under any circumstances, travel with a tour company in an RV again.

"But we've never been to Mardi Gras," Michael had said as we debated whether to sign up for the rally. "You know the company does a good job of planning. We'll have the best grandstand seats for every parade we see. I'm really interested in that Cajun cooking school, and I know you've always wanted to take a steamboat ride on the Mississippi. This trip includes both those things."

"Yeah, but we won't fit in with those people," I said. "Remember the Alaska trip, how we found some of our fellow travelers so . . . so . . ."—I fumbled to find the right word—"conservative?" I said, finally.

We discussed Mardi Gras for another week and finally signed up for the rally. Why not? We'd never been to Mardi Gras before and most likely would never go again.

⌂

Those eight days of Mardi Gras, in retrospect, felt snake-bitten. We got along okay with the folks in our tour group, though we failed to make any friends or add a new contact on Facebook. We found the leaders difficult and dictatorial. For example, rather than letting the bus seating arrangements sort themselves out each day, a co-leader came up with the idea of having everyone draw a playing card, with the suit and number indicating the side of the bus and the row number. After everyone sat down, the woman then walked down the aisle to retrieve the cards to use again for the next trip. Michael misplaced his card, and this leader scolded him like he was six years old.

Another time, as we walked with our group on a downtown sidewalk, this same leader didn't think Michael was walking fast enough.

"Hurry up," she'd said as she pushed him on the back with her palm. "You're going too slow."

The final incident that made me bristle happened when we arrived five minutes early to a designated rendezvous spot. Three of the four leaders waited for us. "Where have you been?" one of them yelled at us as we approached. "Everyone's already headed back to the bus." Her critical, chastising tone was unmistakable.

I exploded. "We're five minutes early. If you wanted us back earlier than this, why didn't you say so?" Michael and I both fumed as we stalked behind them back to the bus.

We saw more parades and collected more beads than either of us ever wanted. Somehow, bead contagion overcame us both. Like an idiot, I found myself bouncing on my feet, both hands in the air, screaming at every passing float. "Here, here," I'd yell. Everyone around us did the same. Each day we'd return home with more of the useless strands and trinkets. On the last night of the rally, at a campground group farewell supper, I tried to give our beads away. No one wanted them. Even the folks who had talked continuously about how much their adorable little granddaughters would love these brightly colored necklaces didn't want any more.

We found the Cajun Cooking School class interesting, but neither of us would eat the crawfish. Learning the things lived in tunnels in the ground, like worms, freaked me out. Later that week, I discovered crawfish mounds in the sandy soil outside the state park office. "Yikes," I'd said to Michael. "Think someone in our group would be interested in digging these up and cooking them for dinner? Maybe we should tell folks where they could find them."

"Be nice," Michael said.

We ate out several times in New Orleans. Although I don't care for spicy, Cajun seasonings, I fell in love with potatoes boiled in Crab Boil. This was a local, specialty seasoning used to cook many different foods, not just crabs.

Eight days of Mardi Gras exhausted us. It reminded me that Michael and I were too old to party like this anymore. Along with about half the people in our group, I'd gotten sick about halfway through the rally. Not real sick, just congested and tired. Not having a thermometer with us, I didn't know whether I ran a fever or not. I wasn't sick enough to miss any of the planned activities, although a couple of other folks in the group did. Michael never caught whatever I had.

We stayed an extra day in the park after the rally ended. During this downtime, Michael caught up on the national news. The little virus in China that we vaguely remembered hearing about in early February had appeared in Seattle, Washington. Scientists were now predicting a 'pandemic,' a word that had no meaning for me. A pandemic was something one read about in science fiction books.

The local New Orleans media described the 2020 Mardi Gras as disastrous in terms of safety. Tandem float accidents killed two bystanders, something that'd never happened before. In both incidents, folks had tried to cross the street by stepping over float tongues. In both cases, the victims had tripped and fallen, and the float tires had crushed and killed them.

No one could have predicted there would be hundreds of more deaths in New Orleans in the next few weeks. The pandemic erupted in New Orleans a week after we left, and scientists were quick to blame Mardi Gras for spreading the virus.

⊟⊡⊟

Scientists finally named the disease caused by this new coronavirus, Covid-19. Soon news sources talked of little else. For a while, Seattle was the only U.S. hotspot. Then New York City began making the hourly news as well. The disease became a killer. No one had ever seen anything like this before.

The explosion of coronavirus cases in New Orleans continued. Speculation soon became scientific data that Mardi Gras—with its hundreds of thousands of tourists packed shoulder-to-shoulder on the streets, in grandstands, in restaurants and bars—caused the outbreak. As we stood in the crowds and yelled for float riders to throw beads our way, potentially infected people all around us spread coronavirus particles through their exhalations, their spit, their coughs and sneezes, and in the things they touched. Uninfected and oblivious people, like Michael and I were at that time, were in close enough proximity to inhale those particles and get sick.

Later, Michael read of a Mardi Gras float rider who was very sick while riding the float and later diagnosed with Covid-19. In the interview with the news reporter, he admitted that he'd been sick during the parade but rode the float anyway. He'd paid several thousand dollars to participate in Mardi Gras and didn't want to lose the opportunity. He admitted that every strand of beads he tossed probably had coronavirus particles on it.

I cringed to think I might have caught one of those infected trinkets.

I didn't think much at the time about my having gotten sick while in New Orleans. Later, when scientists began to report that sometimes cases of Covid-19 are mild, it crossed my mind that maybe I'd had one of those mild cases. Not possible, I told myself, not when these other people in our group also got sick, and all but two of us continued getting on the bus for Mardi Gras outings every day. What were the odds that every single one of us could have had one of those 'mild cases?'

Michael never caught whatever I had, and my symptoms disappeared within a week. I chalked my congestion and fatigue up to a common cold and didn't give it further thought.

A month or so later, in response to one of my Mardi Gras Facebook posts, a friend in Tampa raised the question—on Facebook for the entire world to see—of whether I might be an 'asymptomatic carrier' of the virus. What? Where did she come up with that? My friend had been paying closer attention to newly released medical information about the coronavirus than I had. Not long after her snarky response to my post, CNN began talking about asymptomatic carriers. Suddenly, every stranger on the street became a potential threat. Maybe I was dangerous, too. Maybe I was spreading the coronavirus everywhere I went. I discarded the notion when I realized Michael had not gotten sick. The odds were infinitesimally small that we could both be asymptomatic carriers. I discarded the possibility.

Covid-19 cases in New Orleans skyrocketed. The mayor shut down all nonessential businesses, including the bars and restaurants on Bourbon Street, the street we'd walked up and down many times during our eight days in New Orleans. We read and listened with horror to reports of huge water rats now roaming the streets. The rats had always been around but had scavenged at night in garbage cans behind the food establishments. Now, they brazenly scurried down Bourbon Street in broad daylight, probably driven by hunger and most likely wondering what had happened to their previously plentiful garbage cans full of food.

About three weeks after we left, we heard that the Governor of Louisiana had deployed 400 National Guard reservists to New Orleans. The federal troops evacuated the Bayou Segnette State Park, where Michael and I had just spent nine nights, to set up emergency shelters to house homeless Covid-19 patients.

"I can't believe we were just there," I said to Michael. "This Covid-19 situation has suddenly become very personal."

"Yes, this is a little too close to home. We've got to start paying more attention to the news."

"It's too scary," I said. "Maybe we should go back home."

"No, I don't think we need to do that. Let's just keep listening to the daily updates and be more careful. We'll be okay."

Like everybody we knew, we blithely assumed the government would step in, take control, and return things to normal. After all, we lived in the most powerful and resourceful country on the planet.

I think we both clung to our nonchalance at the beginning of this pandemic. After all, we were on our maiden voyage in our brand-spanking-new 33-ft. Class A motorhome, and we were having a blast. A silly little virus from China wasn't going to make us change our plans.

CHAPTER 4

WALTZING ACROSS TEXAS

When we eased out of Louisiana to head for Texas, the tone of our travel changed. Every couple of hours, we'd listen to CNN news on Sirius radio. Top-of-the-hour stories led with coronavirus updates. Covid-19 cases were popping up all over the country, and New York City sounded like it was on the verge of a meltdown. During the times we weren't listening to the radio, we'd talk about what we'd last heard, trying to figure out if this pandemic would affect us and, if so, how. I fought to keep a pall from descending.

We arrived in San Antonio at the end of February and planned to stay four nights. According to the local news, San Antonio had nine diagnosed cases of Covid-19 on the day we arrived, and the infected patients were all soldiers who had flown internationally. Doctors had isolated them in a hospital at Lackland Air Force base. We sighed in relief that we'd not need to be concerned.

The next night, Michael lobbied hard for us to go to a San Antonio Spurs National Basketball Association (NBA) game at the AT&T Arena, which was only a couple of miles from our RV park. The Spurs would play the Orlando Magic, which was almost like a home team for us since we were from Tampa.

"Do you realize how starved I am for sports?" My husband gave me a hang-dog expression. "I haven't seen a live sporting event since we left home. We could almost walk to the arena."

I finally agreed, despite the exorbitant price of $90 for each ticket. We drove to the arena, paying another twenty bucks for parking. The evening became even more expensive when we added hamburgers and beer to the tab for our dinner. We shared a table with four Puerto Rican women who were out for a night on the town. The fun we had talking and drinking with them almost made the night worth the expense.

The AT&T Arena, with a capacity of 18,581, was about two-thirds filled that night. The excitement was palpable, and the Spurs managed to pull off an eleventh-hour win (114-113) over the Magic. Even I had jumped to my feet and yelled towards the end of the game. It was exciting to have the scores so close, with tension up until the finish. Perhaps because we'd been surrounded by Spurs fans in the stand, I abandoned my allegiance toward the Magic and rooted for the Spurs.

The next day, in deference to my wishes since I'd gone to a basketball game the night before, we went to the San Antonio Botanical Gardens. After a couple of hours strolling through beautiful landscapes, we headed for the Riverwalk. Too tired to do much walking, we went upstairs to the Mad Dogs British Pub for a couple of beers. We laughed and talked with the young couple sitting next to us. Our saucy, attitudinal bartender made folded butcher paper hats with lewd sayings on them for us to wear. I might have had another couple of drinks and laughed a little louder at her jokes if I'd known we were almost at the end of our freedom to drink and laugh in a bar.

By the time we got back to the rig later in the afternoon, San Antonio had exploded with coronavirus updates and warnings. Cases seemed to be increasing exponentially by the hour.

"Wow," I said. "Maybe we shouldn't have been out galivanting around so much this afternoon."

"Nah, we're good," Michael said. "Spurs are playing the Charlotte Hornets tonight. Want to go to another basketball game? We'd have another great evening."

"Nope. I'm tired. One basketball game a weekend is more than enough." I paused. "Maybe even one game a season is enough. Although, I'd choose basketball over football or baseball any day of the week."

As we watched ABC News a bit later, I commented, "Aren't you glad we aren't at that basketball game tonight? I'd be scared to death."

Apparently, many San Antonians had felt the same way I did. Michael and I watched the game on television that night and were amazed to see only a handful of people in the stands. All I could say was, "That's incredible!" The uptick in coronavirus cases in San Antonio had caught the city's attention.

Two days later, on our last day in San Antonio, we made a final trek down the Riverwalk. Hardly anyone had ventured out, and most of the businesses were empty of customers. How quickly things had changed.

As a new author of a book about RVing, *The Reluctant RV Wife*, I'd developed a marketing strategy of contacting activities directors at RV resorts along our route and scheduling book presentations and signings. I'd arranged two presentations in the Big Bend area of southwest Texas and the second one in Austin a couple of weeks after Big Bend. We had a friend in Austin, also a published author, and he'd sold quite a few books in the resort where we planned to stay. I hoped I'd be as lucky.

Not really thinking, and long before either of us realized how much impact the coronavirus would have on our lives, I talked with the activities director at our San Antonio KOA before we left. Spring Break was coming up, and the activities director said the campground would be at capacity. She loved the idea of a humorous RV travel presentation to add to the park's activities during Spring Break. She also managed to find a site for us to stay for a couple of nights before heading up to Austin. We juggled reservations so I could fit in both presentations.

Feeling relief at leaving Covid-stricken San Antonio, we headed out for the almost 500 miles between San Antonio and the Big Bend National Park in Terlingua, Texas. We planned to stay in the Big Bend area for nine days and visit both the national and the state parks. I'd give my first RV resort presentation on March 10th in nearby Lajitas. It would be a small park where I could work out any kinks and bugs. I was super-excited about this opportunity.

If I'd known internet service would be so poor, I'd never have agreed to go to this remote, God-forsaken part of Texas. I was working on a second book, and I needed internet service for research. Michael also felt dismayed by our isolation from the mainstream. He'd become a fanatic news follower, and Sirius radio in the car or the RV became our only means of following what was going on in the world. In the Big Bend area folks, acted as if they didn't know or care that a pandemic was raging. Whenever we'd bring up the subject in the RV park or other places, we received blank stares or shrugs.

On our second day in Big Bend, my phone rang.

"Hello, Gerri. This is Christie from the La Hacienda RV Resort in Austin. I'm calling with bad news. Our corporate office has canceled all scheduled activities because of the coronavirus. We won't be able to let you do your book presentation after all. I'm sorry."

"Jeez," I said to Michael. "What the hell is going on? If things are going to be shutting down, don't you think we ought to hightail it back to Tampa?"

"Nah," my husband said. "We'll be okay."

Despite my gnawing sense that doom lay around the next bend, we decided to continue with our planned itinerary for the next couple of weeks. If this pandemic reached the magnitude scientists were predicting, this might be the last RV road trip we'd take for the next couple of years. Maybe ever. We were both in our seventies with underlying medical conditions. The daily CNN updates on the coronavirus developments scared the bejesus out of us. We both feared we'd die if we caught the virus.

If I'd had any idea of what lay ahead, I would most definitely have started a daily journal. I might have even reevaluated my lack of a spiritual foundation. Maybe I would have questioned whether existential philosophies would provide enough emotional and intellectual sustenance to carry me through.

Was it in Terlingua where I first bolted upright in bed at 4:00 A.M., unable to go back to sleep because of anxiety? That I first wondered if my husband might be right when he'd call me a psycho? When did this deep, rumbling fear begin to seep into my daily activities?

I'd always tried to consider my mortality regularly. I'd undertake virtual rehearsals, dry runs in my head for the real event. I wanted one of those 'perfect deaths,' the kind the Buddhists talk about in which you're given a warning, when you have time to make amends and atone for mistakes, when you're allowed to show dignity and control until you exhale your final breath.

Medical descriptions of Covid-19 deaths horrified me. The images of patients gasping for air, too tired to breathe on their own, and ending up with tubes jammed down their throats and ventilators doing the inhalations and exhalations were graphic and unsettling.

"Michael, we've got to go home. I don't want to die out here in this God-forsaken desert with the scorpions and rattlesnakes, unable to catch my breath."

"Going home won't help," my husband calmly said.

"But if we get Covid, wouldn't you want to be where we have friends, where people know us? I can't imagine dying thousands of miles from home."

"It won't matter where you are. If you get Covid and can't breathe, an ambulance will drop you off at the emergency room door, someone will rush you into a room, put you on a ventilator, and deposit you in ICU. Chances are, you'll never see another soul—same thing with me. If I get it, you'll be saying goodbye to me at the hospital door. It won't matter one bit where our friends and family are or where we are."

This conversation might have been my first inkling that I'd never go home again. Or maybe an early dawning that I was already home and that I'd better make the best of it. What began as a giddy waltz across Texas was starting to feel more like a slow-moving funeral procession.

CHAPTER 5

GRINGO HONEYMOON

Big Bend National Park filled our souls with wonder. Vast, untouched, rugged—it reinforced how small and insignificant a single life is. It also offered a new perspective on the pandemic, and I renewed my resolve to live as fully as possible while I still could. I wasn't ready to stop seeing such untouched beauty as this.

The park felt primitive, remote. I sensed the folks down here cherished their isolation. Politics, pandemics, and contemporary culture didn't seem to interest or affect them. Somewhat resigned, I shrugged at the lack of internet service, took a few deep breaths, and vowed to enjoy our nine days in South Texas despite the disconnect from anything online. Maybe we'd even become less obsessed with this damned coronavirus. Or better yet, perhaps the thing would go away,

The dry, dusty town of Terlingua offered us quick and easy access to the national park. Texas had given the land to the United States in 1944. The park extended over thousands of acres and included mountains, desert, and occasional pockets of forests. The Rio Grande River served as a natural border separating the park from Mexico.

Although we didn't often plan our trips more than a couple of weeks into the future, this time, we knew we had to make reservations early. Our visit in March would come at the peak of the tourist season. We'd waited too long, however, and found ourselves unable to snag reservations in one RV park for the entire stay. We'd have to change locations after four days and move to another park for the other five days.

We'd read that few people came to Big Bend during the hotter months when temperatures routinely reached 120 degrees during the day. I'd felt like our visit was already too late when the mid-day temperature reached a blinding, searing seventy-five degrees in the desert sun on our first day out. I ended up sunburned, shocked that temperatures in the mid-seventies could feel so intense and burn one so badly. I'd not forget my sunscreen again.

As we planned our Big Bend trip, we were most interested in an advertised trip across the Rio Grande River in a wooden rowboat. According to online information, once in Mexico, we could go to a little village and eat tacos and drink beer before returning to the United States. It sounded quaint and funky, our kind of outing.

There's a 25-year-old Robert Earl Keen song my husband loves. It's called "Gringo Honeymoon." Michael knows many of the words and belts them out at what he considers appropriate times. The sardonic, wry lyrics tell of a newly-wed groom's disappointment in his bride during their honeymoon to Boquillas del Carmen in Mexico. Michael's favorite lines are when the husband says he's found a perfect place and wishes time would stop. The wife then matter-of-factly announces it's time for them to go.

Michael and I had a near-reenactment of the Robert Earl Keen song when we visited Boquillas, the site of Keen's inspiration for those "Gringo Honeymoon" lyrics written in 1994. Our quasi-duplication of Keen's song took place on our first day in the Big Bend National Park. We had not realized we'd be going to the town Keen had memorialized in song.

Our seventy-four-mile drive from Terlingua to Boquillas del Carmen (we learned locals do not usually include the 'del Carmen' in the name), the border-crossing site, took almost two hours. We drove across desert terrain dotted with cacti and small shrubs. While seeing no indication of animal life, I knew the desert teemed with insects and animals able to survive the harsh desert environs. Having been in parts of this same Chihuahuan Desert in Arizona and New Mexico, I knew the climate was especially hospitable for rattlesnakes. I kept expecting to see a yellow diamond-shaped warning sign with a cute little rattlesnake curled up with his forked tongue sticking out.

At the Boquillas Crossing, we parked in a dusty, dirt lot with less than a dozen other cars. We walked across the lot into a dark green, heavily-reinforced steel border-crossing building. Although the large, uniformed guard smiled at the half dozen or so of us Americans waiting to get through, he nevertheless managed to intimidate me. Crossing the border to Mexico suddenly felt a bit scary. The guard's only question as we passed through the gate was whether we had our passports with us.

We trudged down a rocky, dusty trail to the river and found an older Mexican man standing beside a dilapidated wooden boat at the water's edge. It would be our passage into Mexico. It occurred to me that we could easily have waded across the narrow, shallow Rio Grande River into Mexico.

"I'm not going to believe it if that guy introduces himself as Captain Pablo," Michael said.

"What are you talking about?"

"You know, from the Robert Earl Keen song."

But I didn't know. I'd never paid that much attention to the song. Later that day, when I googled the lyrics online, I'd realize our river-crossing was only the first of the song lyrics we would experience. Captain Pablo had charged Robert Earl Keen two bucks for the fare in the mid to late nineties. Our captain charged us five bucks each. But I feel confident that back when Keen reportedly made his frequent trips to Big Bend and this little poverty-stricken Mexican town of Boquillas, the rowboat captain didn't have a cool t-shirt like the one ours wore. We never learned the name of our rower, who appeared to speak no English. His emerald green shirt had bold white letters on the back that read: "Welcome to Boquillas 5th Anniversary International Ferry." I took a photo of his back, realizing I was doing what every American tourist did.

After stepping upon Mexican soil, we faced several choices for getting from the riverbank into town. We could either walk, which was free, or pay another five bucks each to make the trip on a burro, horse, or truck. We chose the burros, thinking it'd be fun and charming. Michael later pointed out that Robert Earl Keen had purchased his donkey ride from a blind old Mexican while we contracted with a guy who appeared in his mid-fifties and seemed to have no visual impairments.

On the one-mile ride to the village, with our escort guiding our mounts, I had a second indication of how intense a winter's sun can be when reflected against an ecru-colored ground of sand and rock. Despite the low humidity and a steady breeze, sweat beaded on my face, and my armpits dampened. My next epiphanic moment came when I realized we could have walked into town much faster than these burros got us there.

As our tired old donkeys stumbled along the rocky, gulley-washed road, Michael's burro took a particularly clumsy step, and Michael lurched forward into a death grip on the saddle horn. Later, during lunch, I noticed dried blood on the back of Michael's hand where his watch stem had gouged and broken the skin.

Our burros reached their holding area outside of town after what felt like a very long trip. I was happy to get off the damned thing but disappointed at not finding any shade. Michael was so relieved to dismount he tipped our guide five bucks, announcing that the guy had "saved his life" by helping him get off the burro. In retrospect, I wasn't sure why I'd thought a donkey ride might be quaint and charming. The reality was awkward, uncomfortable, and ungodly hot.

I was surprised to see that the burro handler who had accompanied us up the treacherous path from the river remained at our sides as we entered the town. I soon realized he intended to be our town handler as well as our burro handler. As he escorted us around the village, he pointed out the police station, the three restaurants, the school, the hospital, and some solar panels that generated electricity for the town. He stopped at one of the many little stands displaying embroidered napkins, cloths, and aprons. Small beaded, wire sculptures of animals sat on the table beside the linens. When he introduced the woman in the stall as his wife,

Michael's sense of obligation must have kicked in. He bought two small five-dollar sculptures, one of a tarantula and the other of a rattlesnake.

I hated even thinking it, but according to my calculations, our guide had just collected twenty-five bucks from us—ten for the roundtrip burro ride, five for the tip when he helped Michael dismount, and now ten for trinkets worth under a dollar. I trailed behind the guide as he led us up yet another parched, unpaved road. Eventually, I stopped. "I have to find shade. I'm too hot," I said to him. I gestured toward one of the restaurants we'd passed to make my request clear.

"That's my house down there," our guide said in his limited, broken English. He pointed toward an adobe in the distance with a red truck in front. He looked disappointed that we didn't want to keep walking but shrugged and turned back toward the town's center.

We ate a lunch of tacos and drank beer at the Jose Falcon Restaurant, established in 1973. The restaurant's owner came over to our table (as she did to all the other tables with customers), introduced herself, and left us with a plastic-encased printout telling the story of this restaurant her father had opened when she was a baby. She had grown up in the family business, and it had thrived until 2001. When the 9-11 terrorist attack occurred and the Twin Towers went down in New York, officials closed the border and didn't reopen it until 2013.

Jose Falcon's daughter said she didn't remember seeing or meeting Robert Earl Keen but knew his "Gringo Honeymoon" song. She swore to us that Keen wrote the song on the same outdoor patio where we now sat, looking down at the Rio Grande and up at the Chisos Mountains.

I looked at my husband, who now sported an enchanted, dreamy look on his face. As he gazed off into the distance, looking from the restaurant patio with a Modelo in his hand and a plate of tacos in front of him, I couldn't resist.

"I think it's time to go," I said.

Later, when it really was time to go, Michael looked at his dried-blood-smeared hand and said, "I'm not getting back on that thing." He approached our guide, who had sat patiently in a hand-carved Adirondack chair, watching us while we had enjoyed our lunch and the live music on the shaded patio. Michael asked, "Any chance we could get a truck ride back?"

"Truck? You want truck?" Our guide's eyes sparkled. "Wait. Wait here." He rushed off.

"I'm tempted to start walking," I said. "It's not that far."

"Too hot," Michael said. "He'll be back soon."

We stood in the shade, and I kept looking for a red truck to come up the hill to the Jose Falcon Restaurant. After all, our guide had pointed to a house with a red truck out front, saying the house was his. Instead, our guide appeared in a beat-up old black and white Chevrolet. "Ten dollars," he said to Michael. I guessed our previous payment of ten bucks for a roundtrip burro ride was not transferable to a truck. I sighed.

On the bumpy one-mile ride back to the river, the guide kept saying something to Michael that I couldn't understand from the back seat. When we got down to the river, Michael turned to me and said, "He says he needs five more dollars, that the ten wasn't enough. You got a five?" I rummaged in my fanny pack and pulled out the bill.

Later, on our walk back to the border patrol on the Big Bend side of the river, I said to Michael, "You realize that guy made forty dollars off us today? What a scam."

"Not a scam, just business. It's how the town exists."

I knew that and understood it. But it didn't mean I liked it.

"I felt like we were being guarded. We could have been in Cuba, for God's sake. That guy never took his eyes off us. What'd he think we might do?"

"Maybe they've been trained to look out for terrorists," Michael said. "A lot of Americans hate Mexicans these days. Just think of what our President has said about them, all the names he's called them."

We had to wait in a longer line at border patrol to get back into the United States than the one leaving it. The same border agent was on duty, assisting us individually at the kiosks for automatic scanning and verification of our passports. With each passport scan, a phone at the kiosk rang. Each returning American had to lift the phone and itemize the items he brought back into the country and swear that he wasn't importing drugs.

As I stood at my kiosk passport scanner, I realized the residents of Boquillas could not cross borders the way we Americans so easily did. A citizen in Boquillas del Carmen could not have crossed the Rio Grande River, walked up to border patrol, and entered this country, even with a passport.

We drove off from the crossing area, electing to make one more stop in this remote end of the park for a view of the Boquillas Canyon. When we arrived at the lookout point, we saw two small tables of trinkets like the tarantula and rattlesnake figurines we'd bought from our guide's wife in the village. A little sign indicated the cost of the various items on display, and a small jar sat beside the sign for visitors to leave money for their purchases.

Michael and I later learned the locals called these displays 'honor stores.' Boquillas del Carmen's residents would sneak across the river at night, risking arrest and detainment, and leave their wares to sell. It was yet one more way the dirt-poor residents of the village struggled to survive. Park rangers and border patrols reportedly knew of the illegal crossings but chose to ignore them.

It took a few hours for me to register the political ramifications of our day-trip into this little Mexican town. The town's sole reason for existence was to provide tourists a glimpse at Third World living. For me, the experience sucked. I felt embarrassed to have seen the poverty, the groveling to get our money, and the near desperation in the eyes of the women in the stalls with their embroidered linens and sculpted figures. I hated to have put our guide in the position of asking for more money when we chose not to ride our burros back down to the river.

By the next day, I'd concluded that our guide deserved every penny of that forty bucks the day had cost us.

Robert Earl Keen wrote a powerful song with a universal message that resonates twenty-five years later. Perhaps when Keen made his frequent trips to Boquillas in the nineties, the village really had felt like a place where he could stay forever. I can only hope that if Michael had been Robert Earl Keen and I'd been the new bride, I might have been more sensitive to my new husband's feelings.

As it turns out, in 2020 and after twenty-eight years together, I am happy my husband was able to reenact Robert Earl Keen's excursion into Mexico. I suppose I should feel thankful that he had also realized his dream that we travel in an RV to have these kinds of experiences. But I now wonder—should I feel guilty for profiteering from the trip by writing about it? I'm not sure Robert Earl Keen would have dared to write this song in the current political environment.

Although I found our Gringo Honeymoon day trip into impoverished Mexico interesting and enlightening, I now felt like an ugly American for having gone and gawked. A repulsive one.

CHAPTER 6

TOURISTS NO MORE

As Michael struggled each day to hear coronavirus updates, most of the folks in the Big Bend RV Park acted as if they'd never heard about the pandemic. We tried to do the same. We blithely shopped in the town's small grocery store, long before doctors recommended masks. We drank beer and wine in The Starlight Café, a famous haunt where musicians like Willie Nelson and Robert Earl Keen worked on new material, far away from the fans who would hound them back in Austin, and we laughed and talked with other barroom patrons. We went to the nicest Tex-Mex restaurant in town, the La Kiva, and split a ribeye steak, never dreaming it'd be the last sit-down restaurant meal we'd have for months, maybe even in our lives. We didn't know as we moved about in the little town of Terlingua that it'd be the last time we'd move so freely and with so little anxiety for at least a year, maybe even longer. If I had known, I'd have whooped it up big time.

We'd spent time in the Chihuahuan Desert in both New Mexico and Arizona, and I'd found myself enchanted. The Georgia O'Keefe Ghost Ranch stories from Abiquiu, New Mexico, left me yearning to find a 'spiritual home,' as O'Keefe had found in the New Mexico desert.

However, a couple of weeks in the Chihuahuan Desert in the Big Bend area may have changed my mind about the appeal of desert living. While the beauty of the area took my breath away, the harshness sent chills down my spine. It felt like a million acres of danger. The weather ranged from freezing, snowy winters to occasional torrential rains that drowned unsuspecting tent-campers to searing summer temperatures of over one-hundred-and-twenty degrees with water sources many miles apart to a wind that blew strong and hard year-round. The rocky, craggy, cavernous terrain included near-sea level lows to 8,000-ft. mountainous heights.

Hiking and remote camping in the national park included inclines and declines, slippery gravel, rocks, uneven trails, and no shade until canyons and crevices appeared. Hikers had to know the flora, for some of the native cacti had needle-sharp thorns laden with painful neuro-toxins should they puncture the skin. Hikers also needed to know the fauna, as it was even more potentially dangerous than the plants. Carnivorous predators such as Mexican Black Bears, panthers, coyotes, and mountain lions could eat one alive, and venomous rattlesnakes, tarantulas, and scorpions could kill with bites and stings without timely medical care.

Apologies to the small towns of Terlingua and Lajitas in the Big Bend, but I wouldn't count on the adequacy or timeliness of medical care in this part of the world. The nearest town with even a small hospital was Alpine, Texas, eighty-three miles and a ninety-minute drive to the north. The hospital had twenty-five beds. Hats off to the hardy folks who do the backcountry hiking and camping and to those who boondock in these national and state parks. I admire their trust and confidence that nothing bad will happen, or if it did, that they'd be able to deal with it.

We pulled into an RV resort in Lajitas in early March. We had moved this distance of a mere 17 miles from Terlingua because the Terlingua park had filled its sites with reservations. It was a scary ride in our Class A motorhome with a car in tow, especially when we'd look down at steep drop-offs with no guardrails and no easement beside the pavement. We were lucky to get a back-in site with full hookups. Cable, unfortunately, was not in the cards for us, to Michael's dismay. CNN now reported coronavirus news and little else, and Michael zealously followed every update.

"What's happening to you?" I asked. "You're nothing but doom and gloom these days, with all this virus talk."

"You don't understand, Little Cherrie. It's a pandemic, and I don't think our lives are ever going to be the same again."

"For God's sake, stop calling me Little Cherrie. That's not my name, and I'm certainly not little."

Michael just smiled.

From Terlingua, we had explored the Big Bend National Park. From Lajitas, we planned to explore the Big Bend State Park. A narrow, winding, mountainous State Road 177 connected Terlingua to Lajitas. This state road was the only paved road going through the state park, and it followed the Rio Grande River along the Mexican border. Trails for hiking, mountain-biking, ATVing, and four-wheeled, off-road exploring led off from this one main highway.

In many spots along State Road 177, one could wade across the Rio Grande's ankle-deep water and step into Mexico. Or someone in Mexico could walk to the United States illegally by walking through this same water. In looking at the geography on the Mexican side of the river, the likelihood of anyone being able to survive on foot for the weeks it would take to hike to the river seemed impossible. While no one asked my opinion, I believed the United States would waste a lot of money building a wall along this border.

"So, what's a golf course doing in the middle of the desert?" I asked my husband. We'd arrived in Lajitas, and I was on my iPad, reading about the area. Black Bill's Crossing Golf Course popped up as the number one thing to do.

"Guess people like the weather down here," Michael said, "and folks could probably play golf year-round."

"I can't believe how brutal the sun feels even when the temperatures are in the low seventies." Even though we were in Lajitas at the peak of tourist season, the state park felt empty. We could drive for miles without seeing other vehicles and only occasionally saw anyone on the trails.

"I thought this area was in a severe drought. Where do they get the water to keep grass green for a golf course?" I asked.

"Maybe they play on the dirt."

"I want to see this golf course. From what I've seen of the area so far, they'd need to either bring in fill dirt to cover up all the rocks or spend a tremendous amount of time and money clearing the land enough for a golf course." I realized as I said the words that these kinds of resorts attracted folks with more money than I could imagine having.

Several newspapers and golfing magazines had ranked Black Bill's Crossing Golf Course as the best course in Texas. It offered a combination of mountain, canyon, and desert holes. Reviewers described it as a "bucket list golf course." We had passed an international airport on the outskirts of Lajitas, and I could easily envision corporate jets flying employees to this remote resort area for business meetings or rewards for their high-performing employees.

"Hope we'll be able to find things to do," I said. "Bet everything's going to be pricey." While golf was the major attraction at this resort, Michael and I would not be playing golf. It was not our thing.

Pricey proved an understatement, and I found myself unable to pull the trigger on all but one of the offerings. Options for excursions included zip line tours; four different gun-shooting packages; horseback rides that included champagne, cheese, and crackers; and Jeep rentals for off-road adventures. An adventure tour company out of Terlingua offered stand-up paddle boarding and kayaking trips down the Rio Grande. Trails for mountain-biking and hiking were available to anyone paying the $5.00 daily park admission. However, one had to bring his bicycle since rentals were not available.

As guests of the resort in the RV park, we could have gone to the fitness room for free, purchased a wide variety of services at the Agave Spa, eaten in the resort dining hall, drank in the resort saloon, or spent our money in any of the pricy little shops along the boardwalk. The resort had a theater, but we never saw anything scheduled while we were there.

The tour Michael and I both wanted was Dining Under the Stars, but it had sold out. On the tour, staff took guests in Jeeps high into the backcountry hills and served meals cooked in Dutch ovens over an open fire.

Lajitas was in a black night region, and star-gazing was our neighbors' favorite activity in the RV park. However, our timing seemed to be bad for seeing stars. A full moon combined with a cloud cover blocked the stars for the first two nights of our stay. Michael was beginning to question whether he'd ever see the Milky Way, despite several trips out west, specifically with that mission in mind.

The cloud cover finally broke on our third night in Lajitas. We sat outside that night and saw more stars than we'd seen in years.

"Hey, before we leave here," I said, "I'd like to see that golf course that's gotten international reviews. Let's rent one of those golf carts for twenty-five bucks and take a look." We did, taking turns driving through the famous Black Bill's Crossing Golf Course. We followed the signs and saw all eighteen fairways and holes. The golf cart trail made sharp turns, went up and down steep grades, and crossed two small streams. We saw incredible scenes of mountains, rock formations, and breathtaking natural beauty in addition to the golf course.

"I could understand someone spending a lot of money to fly down here to play golf," Michael said. "It's really impressive."

"Yeah, almost makes me want to take up golf," I said. But I didn't mean it.

Looking back, I wondered if the empty quietness of Lajitas had been related to the coronavirus. Although this was long before masks, social distancing, and business shutdowns, I could feel a growing anxiety. Maybe Michael felt it, too. Perhaps unconsciously, we were already moving away from others, socially distancing, and turning inward. We had considered eating at the resort clubhouse a couple of times, but for some reason, did not. Our most daring people-mingling was having a couple of beers one afternoon at an open-air bar next to the restaurant. We chatted with the bartender. We'd probably have talked to other customers, had there been any.

Our days turned into lazy ones. We tried to walk at least an hour each day, but the steep, rocky, gravelly paths in the desert sun wore us out. We'd return from our walks and spend two hours resting in the air-conditioned RV, trying to recover.

I'd envisioned this downtime as perfect for writing, organizing cell phone photos into albums, and catching up on email communication, both with friends and for book-marketing. I wanted to line up book presentations at RV parks along our route as we traveled. None of these things happened. Internet service was so weak I could barely open an email, and I sure as hell couldn't send one.

I sighed at the irony. I looked around the RV park at folks sitting outside in their folding chairs, many doing nothing other than gazing at the desert and talking. A few had books or iPads in their laps, but most just seemed to be relaxing. I didn't know how to do this. I'd go crazy just sitting and doing nothing, and I believed Michael would as well. As I considered our commitment to sell the house back in Florida and go full-time in the RV, I wondered if I would ever be able to shut down mentally and simply sit.

Hindsight tells me we stopped being tourists there in Lajitas. It was our first real experience with isolation. We made one good friend in that RV resort. Four months later, on Facebook, we'd learn he'd died of Covid-19. I thank God that any prescience I might possess didn't come to the surface to foreshadow what would follow. If it had, I might not have had the courage to carry on.

CHAPTER 7

WHERE CAN WE HIDE?

When Michael and I left for the road in February, the coronavirus was nothing more to us than a whisper in the wind. We went blithely along on our planned itinerary. We attended an RVillage Rally in North Florida. We went to the Mardi Gras in New Orleans, where we scarfed up beads and pushed our way through standing-room-only bars to drink and party. In San Antonio, we enjoyed a live basketball game, a crowded Riverwalk, and drinking, laughing, and yelling in an Irish pub. Finally, we arrived in the Big Bend area to experience our first real taste of social isolation.

While in the Big Bend, I'd almost forgotten about the escalating warnings concerning the virus, although Michael continued to get updates on his iPad and fill me in. Still, reading about outbreaks didn't have as much impact as seeing live coverage on TV, which we didn't have in Terlingua and Lajitas.

When we returned to San Antonio, a new world awaited us. We now witnessed a slow exodus out of the KOA park, not the onslaught of families trying to get in for Spring Break that we'd expected. In the activities hall, the laundry room, outside the café where folks gathered for food and drinks, the coronavirus dominated at least fifty percent of all conversations. We debated with others as to whether to change travel plans. We noted that some couples decided to return home sooner than planned while others chose to be extra careful but continued their trips.

We stayed at the San Antonio KOA five nights and watched RV-ers leave daily. Prime Minister Trudeau had called the Canadians back home, warning that their health care coverage would not apply in ten days should they contract Covid-19. Like Florida, Texas attracted a considerable number of Canadians for the winter. It was now mid-March, and although getting close to the end of the winter season, many of those snowbirds complained it was too early and still too cold to go home. We talked with dismayed Canadians who would return to six feet of snow and even more who were angry over the nonrefundable money they'd paid for premium seasonal campsites they now had to abandon.

"The only future I have are doctors' appointments," I said to Michael. "Everything else I'd scheduled to do when we got back home has been canceled. I don't have a future anymore." I could not believe how, in the past two weeks, life had changed. It had gone from looking rosy and positive to looking like a world painted by Stephen King in *The Stand*. Or by Cormac McCarthy in *The Road*.

"My, but you're dramatic. You need to take some deep breaths and calm down."

"Hard to be calm when the entire world has fallen apart. We're down to three rolls of toilet paper, for God's sake, and there's none in the grocery store. What are you going to do, Mr. Cool and Confident, when you don't have anything to wipe your butt with?"

"We'll get toilet paper, Little Cherrie. Just don't you worry your pretty little head."

I hated it when my husband became condescending, and this was exactly how I perceived his comments. I had always viewed myself as the one with common sense in this relationship and him as my impulsive, fly-by-the-seat-of-your-pants partner.

I shrugged. There was nothing I could say that would make sense to him, maybe not even to myself. I remembered the stock market crash and recession of 2008 and how my 403(b) dwindled to half its value.

In retrospect, I was too immature and naïve to understand the consequences of having one's retirement funds disappear. I was working then and not paying much attention to money. It worked out that time, and the money returned. But would it now, in 2020? I was no longer in the work force. What money I had squirreled away was all there'd be. I no longer added to the pot. CNN News reported on the Dow Jones twice an hour, and it seemed to be in freefall. My financial advisor had invested most of my retirement savings in the stock market. This news did nothing to allay my anxieties.

"You know, this KOA is not going to be a good place to be stranded," I said. "Everything's closing down. We need to do something." I ticked off the places local news reported as already closed—the Alamo, the San Antonio Zoo, the botanical garden, and over half the restaurants and bars in town. The rumor was that even the San Antonio Riverwalk would soon be off-limits for pedestrian traffic. The thought of quarantining in an RV in a KOA campground sounded dreadful to me.

"Yeah, I know," Michal said. "We need to find a place to hunker down until this blows over."

"Hey," my excited husband said the next morning, "I've got a great idea. You're looking for new material for another book about RVing, right? A new angle, a new experience, new material of interest to both RVers and non-RVers? I have found the perfect place."

I could tell by the twinkle in his eyes and the grin on his face that my husband had an idea he wouldn't let go, and I could tell by his lengthy, proselytizing introduction that he expected me to resist his proposal. I knew this man well.

"It's stupid to stay in a crowded metropolitan area like San Antonio," Michael said. "This coronavirus thing is going to get worse, and we're going to end up stuck inside this RV." He paused, caught his breath, and threw me a big grin. "Look what's happening in Italy. And now it's popped up big-time in Seattle. This is going to spread all over, and we need to run to a protected rural area so our chances of getting sick will be less."

Around this time, President Trump formed coronavirus task forces while simultaneously assuring everyone the virus would be over in a couple of weeks. He even suggested the Democrats had manufactured fake news about the coronavirus as a ploy to reduce his ratings and hurt his reelection campaign. When the virus cases began multiplying exponentially in New York, Governor Andrew Cuomo started daily briefings. We stayed glued to Cuomo's briefings with almost the same attentiveness as we did CNN's.

"Maybe we should go home," I said. Home was the only place that made any sense to me, but I knew it was not what Michael wanted to do.

Michael dropped teasers for a couple more days before he finally made his pitch. "I've found a really secluded, gated RV park down in the Rio Grande Valley in south Texas. It's out in the country, not too far from Brownsville and San Padre Island, where you've wanted to go anyway. It's also pretty close to the Mexican border. It'd be a perfect place to hole up until this coronavirus outbreak calms down. Maybe they'd even let you do a presentation and sell books there."

"I'm not understanding all this buildup, Michael. What is it that you're not telling me? What's with the long list of perks?"

My charming husband hesitated. "Trust me. You'd get at least one chapter for your next book about RVing if we went to this RV park. It'd be another aspect of RVing that we've heard about but never experienced."

"Come on, Michael. Just spill it."

"It's a place I think we need to check out for a week or so, see what it's like. It'd be something different for us. Something readers would scarf up in a heartbeat. You might be able to sell an entire book based on this one chapter you could write after going there."

I was getting exasperated. "Would you please just tell me what the hell you're talking about and cut out all the verbiage? We've got to get out of San Antonio. What is it about this park that makes you feel the need to sell it to me?"

I wasn't prepared for the answer.

"It's a nudist resort," my husband said.

CHAPTER 8

HELD CAPTIVE BY THE CORONAVIRUS IN A NUDIST RV PARK

"You're a writer of RV travel stories," my persuasive and manipulative husband had said. "A nudist park will get you motivated to write again."

I wasn't as averse to the idea of visiting a nudist park as I pretended to be. I'd done some research on the topic decades earlier out of curiosity. The benefits of being natural and free were easy to understand and accept. I was in my seventies now, no longer self-conscious or embarrassed about much of anything. Still, I made Michael work. I made him needle and wheedle until, finally, I agreed.

"One week, Michael. I'll stay for one week. And if you ever tell any of our friends we went there," I said, "I'll divorce you." I didn't mean it, but I didn't say that to him.

He cast me a triumphant grin. I shot him a bird.

"Just think," Michael said. "We're getting all this laundry done, and these clothes will still be clean a week from now." We were finishing our weekly laundry in San Antonio, getting ready to hit the road for our nudist adventure the next day.

"Dream on, sweetheart. Just because I agreed to go to a nudie park doesn't mean I'm taking my clothes off."

"Oh, you'll take them off," Michael said. "They're pretty clear about the rules down there. It's a nudist park, and that means no one wears clothes."

I rolled my eyes. "Yeah, right."

We arrived at the park entrance to find a locked gate and an intercom. Michael pushed the button, and I cringed as the steel gate inched open. Mercedes, the owner, met us at the park's office, wearing nothing but a scarf around her waist. "You're the last people we're letting in," she said. "This coronavirus has exploded, and we have a lot of older, fragile people living here. I intend to keep my guests healthy."

Once we set the rig up, we sweltered inside the RV for almost an hour as the A/C slowly cooled the interior to a tolerable temperature. Michael had shed his clothes the minute he came inside and had wanted me to do the same. "I'm not ready," I said. "You promised no pressure, remember?"

"While in Rome. . . ." I heard exasperation in my husband's voice.

"Leave me alone! I'll take off my clothes when I'm good and ready."

A bit later in the afternoon, our neighbors to the left returned home in their Jeep. Michael went out to meet them. I followed with reluctance, still clothed.

"We're Robert and Andrea," the man said. "Welcome."

Michael and I both liked them immediately. Robert was tall, fit, and wore his long gray hair in a ponytail. We'd later learn he was part American Indian, a former U.S. Marine, and from a long lineage of religious fundamentalists in Idaho. Andrea talked a mile a minute with a German accent, at times struggling to find the words she wanted in English.

"Andrea speaks five languages," Robert explained. "She worked as a flight attendant for TWA before retiring."

We chatted a few minutes until Robert excused himself, saying they had to put their groceries away. They walked over to their Jeep, and each grabbed a couple of grocery bags. When Robert returned to collect the rest of the groceries, he'd taken off his clothes. His overall bronzed body made me gawk.

An hour later, watching my nude husband outside setting up our Weber-Q grill to cook steaks for dinner, I took a deep breath, ripped off my clothes, and stomped down the RV steps.

"It's my debut," I snarled, glaring at my spouse. "Happy?"

Screeching birds woke us up the next morning with raucous, obnoxious squawks. "What the fuck?" Michael yelled from the bedroom. He typically stayed up until midnight and then slept until eight or nine. I was already up, hunched over my laptop. "Some kind of birds," I said.

We later learned they were chachalacas, fowl in the same family as chickens, turkeys, and pheasants. While I didn't think anybody ate them, the ones in our mesquite tree looked almost the size of turkeys. They were common in the Rio Grande Valley and gravitated to mesquite trees for roosting and mating. Unfortunately for us, spring happened to be their mating season and early morning was their time for friskiness. "Pick me, pick me," they seemed to call to each other.

We would listen to this din several hours every morning during our stay. While we would come to appreciate the mesquite tree for the shade it offered throughout the day, we would not welcome the bird droppings that landed on our grill and picnic table. These were big birds, and they made big poops. We quickly learned to stow our folding chairs when our butts weren't in them.

The following day, we watched a steady stream of walkers make laps around the park. Some walked dogs, others walked alone or with friends. The common element was that they all wore sneakers and nothing else.

"We need some exercise," Michael said. "Let's do a few laps, log in some steps."

"Sure," I said. "Let me put on my UPF-50 shirt."

"You can't go out there wearing a long-sleeved shirt, for God's sake."

"I'm being treated for skin cancer, and I certainly will wear a shirt." A glance in the full-length mirror before we walked outside assured me nothing important showed.

"We are sickly pale compared to all these folks," Michael said. "Before we leave here, I intend to have a tan."

I found it hard not to stare at all the bronzed bodies, identical in overall, uniform color. Only the sizes and shapes differed. "Think these guys hold their penises up when they sunbathe to make sure the underside gets tanned?" I asked.

"Be nice," my husband said.

***

"Happy hour at four tomorrow under the big tree next to the pickleball courts," Andrea called over to me. "Bring your chairs and drinks. We must wear masks, and each couple must sit six feet from the next couple and only ten people to the circle. If a sixth couple joins, we'll just start a new circle."

"How does that work, since we have to wear masks? How are we supposed to drink?" Michael asked.

"We'll see. Maybe we could cut little holes in our masks and sip through straws."

"I'm thrilled we got invited to this happy hour," I later said to Michael. "This social isolation is getting to me. Maybe we'll make some friends here after all."

"It'll be good to get to know some folks. Doesn't look like we're going to be going anywhere anytime soon."

"I promised you one week here, buddy." I had no place to put my anger and frustration. Given a terrifying virus with alleged wildfire contagiousness had descended, I was at least rational enough to understand we were safer right here in this nudist RV park than we'd be just about anywhere else on the planet. It was rural, isolated, gated, and run by a militant owner hell-bent on keeping the damned virus out of her park.

At the scheduled time, we joined four other couples at the mesquite tree for our first happy hour convergence in the nude. Each couple sat the required distance from the next, and someone had set up a boom box to play classic rock softly in the background. These were folks just like us—same ages, same tastes in music, so many other things in common—except Michael and I generally wore clothes. It appeared the other couples valued that happy hour socialization just as we did. The gatherings became biweekly events.

"It makes sense that Andrea would be a nudist," I said to Michael a few days later. "She's German." I'd been reading online about the naturist movement. While the roots went back to ancient Greece and Rome and to those muscle-marbled, sculpted gladiators who preened in the coliseums, this more recent strain of nudism originated in Germany during the eighteenth century. This thread viewed nudism as part of a larger movement to restore health from disease and malaise. The Germans established colonies where folks could eat natural foods, soak up the sunshine, and catch up on their rest, all in the buff. However, the Germans didn't confine their nakedness to isolated retreats. Per internet postings, every waterfront site where Germans ever congregated became topless zones, regardless of local ordinances.

My curiosity grew as I read. We'd gotten to know Robert and Andrea well enough I felt comfortable asking. "Does swinging go on at this place?" Those loud mating calls of the chachalacas made me think of sex and how nudist parks in Florida had reputations as hotbeds for lewd and decadent behavior.

"Well, I think maybe it happens, but we've never seen it. It'd have to be discreet anyway. Management wouldn't allow it," Robert said.

"Oh, yes," Andrea said. "We have these big dances every Saturday night during the season, and Mercedes is very strict—no lingerie. They don't want this place to get a reputation for swinging or any kind of overt sexuality. It's a family resort, and there are sometimes children here."

The shutdown of Texas continued, and Covid-19 cases skyrocketed. Circular walks around the RV park, happy hours, and occasional chats with other residents became our only outings, except for weekly trips to the grocery store.

We met Sarah, who lived several sites from us down the street, a crone from Arizona who spent four hours every afternoon "doing my inner work." She claimed to be a true and rare empath. "That means I can feel everything other people feel when I talk with them. It's a heavy burden," Sarah said.

"Huh?" I later said to Michael. "Think she could feel that I didn't buy for a minute what she was saying?"

Michael laughed.

We met Carol, Sarah's best friend who lived across the street. Carol was a musician who gave concerts and led sing-alongs at the park. Or at least she had until management shut down all group activities because of the pandemic. One night, Carol led a few of us women in an 8 P.M. howling at the moon activity as a way of showing our solidarity during the crisis and our support for first responders.

We met other folks into alternative practices, like the eighty-year-old from Massachusetts who described herself as a certified aromatherapist who specialized in women's breast health via the application of essential oils, which she happened to sell. Her story produced yet another silent "oh, really" response on my end. It all added up to a bit too much woo-woo in that park for my taste.

I came to view Andrea as the park's busy-body, the one who knew everyone and everything, but in a good way. I liked her a lot. One time I tried to report a conversation I'd overheard on one of my daily walks in which three residents were complaining about one of Mercedes' new rules.

"But who were they?" Andrea kept asking me.

Finally, in exasperation, I said, "I have no idea who they were. They were wearing masks. With all these masks, it's like genital recognition has replaced facial recognition, and I didn't recognize those genitals."

Andrea burst out laughing. "You're so right. I hadn't thought of that before, but the other day I found myself looking at a guy's penis, trying to figure out who he was. Please don't tell Robert."

If I'd entered this nudist RV park with any notion of sexual titillation, that notion evaporated in short order. Having expected at least a little lewd and lascivious flirting, I was surprised to learn that I was one of the youngest people in the park at seventy-two. I saw no evidence of a functioning libido at any time during our stay.

I would have thought nudists prided themselves on svelte, healthy bodies, but again I was wrong. These seventy, eighty, and ninety-year-olds boasted more sags and wrinkles, excess pounds and surgical scars, and 'to hell with it/I don't care attitudes' than I'd ever seen congregated in one place. For the most part, the residents were not newcomers to the au natural scene. They'd been living this lifestyle for decades. Any self-consciousness had vaporized years ago.

The pervasive New Age spiritualism in the park surprised me, but perhaps it shouldn't have. I'd gone through periods of alternative dabbling—sitting in silence for three hours with an avatar in a small village in Germany, dancing around bonfires with pagans, and casting a Medicine Wheel with Sun Bear before he passed away and long before the Indian Nation dubbed him a profiteering phony. I'd meditated with the Buddhists, not realizing until later that osteoarthritis caused my knees to scream in agony with my pathetic approximations to the Lotus pose. I'd thought it'd been my lack of faith. Bottom line: I identified with these folks. I felt I understood them.

I'd always thought of myself as liberal and freer than most in my lifestyle. However, I left the nudist park feeling like a charlatan, an imposter, a poser, as much of a phony as the world now viewed Sun Bear. Even worse, I'd gone into this park as a voyeur to collect anecdotes and experiences for new chapters in an in-process manuscript. In other words, to pander to the public. I hadn't entered the park as a nudist, and I didn't leave the park as one. It was a great relief to put on clothes as we packed to leave. My nipples had been sore for weeks, and a bra had never felt so good.

The nudist immersion left a disconnect between how I'd previously viewed myself with my new insight that I was an imposter. The guests at the nudist park were the ones who'd searched, found something, and stuck with it. They hadn't spent decades playacting with various isms and checking out the latest trends. Why hadn't anything stuck with me the way it had with these folks?

But maybe it wasn't an issue of nothing sticking. Michael and I had wrestled for five years with the RV decision of whether to go full-time. We'd come very close on a couple of occasions to selling the house and living as nomads. But what had ended up stuck in my craw was pure, unadulterated indecision.

Something jiggled loose in my brain after over six weeks in the nudist park, and a sense of urgency took over. Most of the folks in the park were older than we were. The small amount of time we had left hit me square on, especially with the new fear of contracting Covid-19 and dying.

Would these new insights, combined with the raging coronavirus pandemic, finally give me the courage to sell our house in Tampa? I felt ready, but I was afraid to tell Michael. I'd jerked him around once before with a commitment to go full-time, and then I reneged. I couldn't let myself do that to him again. Besides, this virus scared the bejesus out of me, and I didn't want to go back to Florida. It wasn't safe there. The safest place either of us could imagine, given the rising number of cases of Covid-19 and fatalities across the United States, seemed to be our new 33-ft. Thor ACE motorhome. I took it as a sign.

I sighed in relief as the big gate at the park's entrance closed behind us as we pulled out. There were only a few nudist RV parks in this country, and chances were slim we'd run into another one anytime soon. I'd be able to enjoy our upcoming adventures fully clothed. Thank goodness.

CHAPTER 9

REALITY SETS IN

I like change as much as the next person. But like most freedom-loving Americans, I want to be in control of as many of those changes as possible. I watched with both anger and understanding at people's reactions to the pandemic. I understood the refusals to follow CDC guidelines and stay home but simultaneously screamed in rage that they should exercise such freedoms when it puts my life in jeopardy.

I'd studied these kinds of moral conundrums while working towards a social work degree. My graduate program taught that the rights of the group must always come before the rights of individuals. Instructors taught us to employ standards of fairness and justice in all situations. Examples of injustices might be using influence or connections to get someone bumped up on a long waiting list for services, or showing preferential treatment based on criteria not universally applied, or excluding groups of people based on specific characteristics, such as age, race, sex, sexual orientation, political orientation, or whatever. A classic example used in education was allowing one disruptive student to disturb an entire classroom's learning. Put succinctly, the principle required that actions always result in the greatest good for the greatest number. These ideas were a part of my profession's code of ethics, and I'd live and practiced these beliefs my entire career.

But now, dammit, the CDC had made recommendations that would result in the greatest good for the greatest number, but politicians refused to support and enforce the guidelines. The country had gone berserk. There didn't seem to be much I could do other than run for the hills, which we were doing both literally and figuratively. I raged at my helplessness.

I watched state and local governments make half-hearted efforts to contain the coronavirus. At the same time, I clung to my naive hope that the pandemic would end in a couple of months and would have little additional impact on my life. However, a new reality was forming, one which allowed me no input in how it would develop or end. I could wax philosophical into infinity, scream my views of what the leaders should do, but my protestations wouldn't change a thing.

I understood current events enough to know Michael and I couldn't return to Tampa just yet. Travel had become difficult, and some states, including Florida, had imposed quarantines for people crossing state lines. Our RV news sources painted grim travel pictures of canceled campground reservations, closed RV parks, and occasional terrifying stories of RVers stranded and unable to get needed repairs to their rigs so they could continue their journeys.

Michael's take on the coronavirus was different from mine. My generally optimistic husband offered a doom and gloom forecast. As a former respiratory therapist with decades of critical care work in hospitals, he repeatedly lectured me on airborne particles and how they entered and infected the body. I tried to shut my ears. I didn't want to hear his dire predictions, and I certainly didn't want to entertain notions of irreversible changes in my life. I was willing to sit out the pandemic for a few more months out west in our RV if it felt halfway safe, but then, I wanted life to return to normal.

Sheltering in place seemed like the best strategy, but where should we go? While rural south Texas had felt safe and secure for the first month we were there, our anxieties mounted when the Texas Governor ordered businesses to start reopening.

The weather was yet another indication that it was time for us to leave south Texas. It was desert, and April temperatures had already risen above a hundred degrees several times. We were thankful for that damned chachalacas-infested mesquite tree beside the RV because it provided a few hours of shade each day on our tin can house, which made it a bit more bearable. However, we knew we couldn't stay. We'd learned years earlier that RVs had little insulation. Extreme temperatures in either direction created uncomfortableness inside. We'd learned it was easier to warm a cold RV than it was to cool a ninety-degree interior as an unrelenting sun beat down. God had created electric space heaters, and they worked well enough on cold mornings, but for some reason, he'd not yet come up with a comparable, portable supplement for air conditioning. Fans didn't get the job done.

"I've got to get out of this heat," I'd said to Michael. "I'm dying here." We were trying to plan our next stop, knowing we needed to find a spot and stay there for a while.

"Let's maybe go month by month," Michael had said. We poured over our Rand McNally Road Atlas, checked the Weather Channel for temperatures, and tracked Covid-19 cases by state based on CDC incidence reports. We decided to head to New Mexico. We packed up the RV with enough food and water for five days and hurried across virus-infected Texas to Santa Fe. We stopped only for gas and used disposable gloves when touching gas pump handles. We'd made KOA reservations along our route. This campground chain offered RVers safe, contactless check-ins in which an employee met us in a golf cart, handed us our paperwork through the window, and led us to our site.

"I'm a wreck, Michael. I've got a knot in my stomach that just won't go away." We were into the third day of the interminable trip across Texas, a state so large that officials should long-ago have subdivided into at least four states. My anxiety felt like it would explode. On the positive side, there was hardly any traffic on the highways.

"Guess most folks are taking that stay-at-home order seriously," Michael said.

"Yeah, but I am so happy to be getting the hell out of Texas." We'd settled into our campground for the night and were watching the evening news. The Texas Governor wanted his state back to normal. "Texas is not going to be a sanctuary much longer." My prophecy proved correct, and within a couple of months, Hidalgo County, where we'd enjoyed six weeks of relative safety, became the new hotspot for Covid-19 cases in the United States.

"It's like we're getting out of places just before they implode," Michael would say later. "We were in New Orleans for Mardi Gras. We left there, and a couple of weeks later, the pandemic rushed in like a tsunami. We went to San Antonio, went to a basketball game and drank in a pub along the Riverwalk, only to have all hell break loose right after we left. Then we headed to south Texas, and as soon as we left, the coronavirus erupted in Hidalgo County like Mt. Vesuvius. I think we're doing something right, don't you?"

"Just hope we're not asymptomatic carriers, leaving a wake of destruction behind us everywhere we go."

"It'd never happen that we could both be positive with no symptoms. You need to stop worrying about that, Little Cherrie, and just be relieved that we've managed to stay safe so far," my husband said.

We arrived at a different Santa Fe than the one we remembered from a 2019 road trip. We stayed at the same RV park as before, only to find it almost empty and quite rundown. Our check-in would be our first time entering an RV park without any contact with management, not even by phone or a drive-by. While Michael had made our reservations by phone from south Texas a couple of weeks earlier, at check-in we found our paperwork attached to a bulletin board outside a locked office door. This no-contact registration would become a routine procedure at RV parks in the future.

While we found Santa Fe safe enough, there was little to do since almost everything had closed. Also, it was mid-May, and the high desert temperatures were getting hotter by the day. "We can't stay here," I whined to my husband. "Find us a cooler place."

The week-long Santa Fe stopover helped me calm down, however. We could mitigate our social isolation with a couple of well-planned, socially-distanced get-togethers with friends in the area. We reconnected with a couple with whom we'd gone on an Alaska trip in 2017. They were from Santa Fe and had recently relocated to Rio Rancho, an hour south of Santa Fe. We trusted each other enough to enjoy several hours of conversation and dinner in their home one evening. It made me feel like a sociable human again.

Our second social get-together was with Les and Kerry Jones, the new friends we'd met at the RVillage rally in February. We'd stayed in touch via Facebook. They RVed full time and were now serving as Workcampers at the Santa Fe KOA, about ten miles southeast of town. We drove up late one afternoon and had a great time over cocktails and grilled Ribeye steaks.

We might have stayed at this KOA had it not for the lack of Verizon cell phone services. Michael shared his theory with our hosts.

"You know what KOA does when choosing a location for a campground, don't you?" my husband asked. "They pick up their cell phones, and then they start driving out of town. They watch as the number of bars goes from five to four and on down. When the Verizon cell phone bars hit zero, they build a campground."

"Very funny," I said. I'd heard his theory before many times. I don't think Les and Kerry found Michael's conclusions particularly amusing. However, I think my husband might have been right. For some strange reason, Verizon cell phone service is often poor or nonexistent in KOAs.

While parked in Santa Fe, we again scoured the internet, studied our atlas, and listened to coronavirus updates. We developed a strategy: stick to sparsely populated areas in cooler weather with a low incidence of Covid-19 cases. From Santa Fe, we chose Durango, Colorado, which was a four-hour drive north of Santa Fe. It seemed to fit all our criteria.

I realized we were stumbling in the dark, trying to run from the coronavirus in our RV. Rather than feeling like a part of any group, we felt alone, isolated from our fellow citizens. We moved according to our self-interests, trying to stay safe but not actively helping others, except for wearing masks, socially distancing, and going into stores only for necessities. As a social worker who'd spent forty years working on behalf of others, what we were now doing felt selfish. Lame.

I could only shake my head in wonder that a mere three months earlier, at the RVillage Rally in north Florida, I'd felt so optimistic that we'd find community among RVers. Now I felt we were alone and in the scariest situation I'd ever encountered.

We were thousands of miles from our home in Tampa, Florida, and worlds removed from our everyday routine. We'd arranged with our next-door neighbor to look after our house for two months when we'd left Florida in mid-February. We'd now been gone over three months. I felt like we'd become fugitives without having done anything wrong.

We had decisions to make. I did not like our new reality one bit, but I finally accepted its truth.

CHAPTER 10

THE WRESTLING MATCH

"You realize I can't go back to Florida," Michael said. We'd left Santa Fe and were about halfway to Durango, bouncing along in our motorhome, happy to be on the way to our next destination. "I'd die if I got Covid-19. We're a lot safer in this RV, where we can change the view outside our windows from time to time, where we can pick sparsely populated places with good weather and low rates of the virus."

"I can't do it, Michael. I'm not ready to give up my life." Tears filled my eyes. He won't go back to Florida? I thought. Under any circumstances? He wants us to live in the RV indefinitely, or at least until this pandemic is under control?

"It'll be over soon, Little Cherrie. Scientists all over the planet are working in overtime to develop a vaccine."

"It may never end," I said. "Think of all the diseases for which vaccines have never been developed—Dengue Fever, AIDS, Malaria, even hookworms, for God's sake. What makes you think there'll be an effective vaccination for Covid-19 in our lifetimes?"

"Regardless of a vaccine, I don't think you're hearing what I'm saying. I'm a seventy-year-old Type 1 diabetic with a compromised immune system. If I caught this virus, I wouldn't survive."

"You can't know that."

"Of course I can know that. It's my body."

"So, you're just taking over, making all the decisions?" I couldn't believe my husband was so adamant and uncompromising.

"If there's not a cure or vaccine, we'll just spend the rest of our lives as nomads," Michael said. "We'll stay in remote areas, find weather we like, and just relax. What would be wrong with that?"

I glared at him. Had we not been on the road, I'd have stomped down the steps and slammed the door behind me. His words stunned me. I seethed in silence. He'd never issued an ultimatum like this, a unilateral statement of what he would or wouldn't do. He'd rankled my feminist dander, big time. The thought of leaving him with his damned RV crossed my mind.

But what would be wrong with spending the rest of my life reading, writing, and relaxing? We'd been on the road almost three months already, a month longer than we'd intended. We couldn't have made it back to Tampa. RV parks across the country had shut down. We were stuck.

I had to admit life on the road in the RV was easy. Uncomplicated. Few demands and hardly any responsibility. Michael and I got along well enough, probably as well as possible after living together for almost thirty years. I had enough privacy, enough personal space. I didn't think I'd ever feel bored. I could entertain myself watching tree leaves blow in the wind. There'd been many times when it'd crossed my mind that life on the road made more sense than maintaining a big house, a pool, and a manicured yard.

I had to remember, too, that we'd upgraded to this bigger RV for a reason, and the reason was to go full-time. We were on our maiden voyage to identify the factory flaws in the RV. I'd committed to becoming a full-time nomad. The RVillage Rally just three months ago had strengthened that promise. But having my spouse unilaterally announce what he would and wouldn't do was unacceptable on many levels. Wasn't marriage supposed to be a partnership, a sharing of ideas, and a compromise when the two parties wanted something different?

I fumed. If I'd reneged on a promise one time about going full-time, I sure as hell could do it again. I felt like my husband had just pushed me out onto a frozen pond, one with fragile ice. Machismo proclamations did not impress me one bit.

We'd been RVing for almost five years. In the beginning, I'd kicked, screamed, and resisted leaving my garden, my 200+ orchids, my Toastmaster clubs, my writer groups, and my friends and neighbors. Each RV trip seemed to last a little longer, and we'd spent as much as six months on the road. I'd adjusted and had even grown to appreciate and enjoy a gypsy lifestyle.

But did I have the courage to leave my real life behind? Would I hate my husband forever if I gave in to his ultimatum? What was a marriage anyway? I used to think Michael was my soulmate. Now I wondered. How could someone in a long-term relationship like ours arbitrarily announce he wouldn't go home again? He was effectively giving me the finger, discounting my preferences.

We'd reached a stalemate. I think he knew better than to bring the subject up again anytime soon. The topic lay dormant for the next couple of weeks.

I couldn't let it go. What does it mean when one's spouse tells you he'll die if he catches a highly contagious virus? Is it the ultimate emotional blackmail, or is it a legitimate medical concern? Michael is younger than I am but has medical and orthopedic issues. He can't do some of the activities he could do three years ago. Sometimes, I wanted to scream at him to try harder, walk faster, lift and twist, and bend to do all the things he once did on autopilot. I felt guilty that thoughts like these even crossed my mind. Although I tried hard to mask my frustrations and fears, I knew my husband sensed my disappointment that we were no longer able to do some of the things we used to do. I also knew his anger and frustration were more profound than mine and had nothing to do with me.

I didn't think I'd die if I caught Covid-19. I believed I'd get sick, and then I'd recover. What if Michael and I were both sick at the same time?

He's said, "A hospital is the last place I'd want to go if I get sick. Promise me you won't call 9-1-1."

"You're crazy," I'd said. "You want me to sit in this RV and watch you die? Not going to happen. I'll call an ambulance if you get that sick."

"I suppose you'd have to. Oh, well . . . It was just a thought."

Yes, it was. Now he could forget it.

How can you know whether you'll be strong enough when something bad happens? Situations and circumstances create the heroes, not some internal, untapped reservoir of strength and exceptionality. One can never really know how they'd react or hold up until the crisis arrived.

During this quiet interim, during which I felt the heavy weight of this death conversation, my entire future seemed suspended. I remembered my earlier insights that all my belongings were weighing me down, preventing me from growing, expanding, experiencing. I considered my seventy-two years, my compromised lungs from years of smoking, and all the little red flags that were popping up and suggesting major health issues down the road in my poor old aging body. What was there about my life in Tampa, Florida, that I clung to so desperately? What made me afraid of change, afraid to take the risk of spending a couple of years doing something different? Like living in this blankety-blank RV, for example.

Except it was no longer the blankety-blank RV. It had become home. Being stuck in this small motorhome at the outbreak of a pandemic made me feel safer and more secure than anywhere else I could imagine. My world had shrunk, and now everything essential for my survival lay within an arm's length. With everything outside feeling dangerous, the inside of this coach had become an oasis, a refuge from the storm, a perfect place to hunker down. Withdrawal from this frenetic, pandemic chaos and a return to a simple, barebones lifestyle—one with a greatly reduced likelihood of getting sick and dying—made perfect sense.

I also realized I'd be as likely to die from Covid-19 as my husband was. My magical thinking was not going to change one thing about the damage I'd done to my body through the years or the genetic whammies my parents had tossed me. I needed to get off my high horse and admit I was as vulnerable as the next person, more vulnerable than many, and probably equally as vulnerable as my husband.

Three weeks after my husband's announcement that he wouldn't go back to Florida, I brought the subject up again.

"I'm ready to do it," I said. We sat in our lovely campground in Durango, looking out at pastures, horses, and snow-capped mountains. Temperatures dipped to the mid-forties at night and climbed to the upper seventies during the day. We'd found several easy hiking trails, a never-crowded grocery store, and I'd even bought a geranium to sit and look pretty on our picnic table. We'd made friends with a couple of the neighbors. I was writing again. I felt more relaxed than I'd been in decades.

"I'm finally there," I continued. "This can be my life, and it will be all I'll need for a couple of years. It'll be an experiment—to see how it changes me, to give me new material to write about, and to gain more credibility as an RVer. And more importantly, it'll give you the chance to live your dream of living on the road. I'm ready to sell the house."

As I said this, I realized the house had been my security blanket, my ace-in-the-hole, my 'out' should things go wrong or if I changed my mind again. Selling the house was the most irreversible decision I'd ever made. Sure, there could be other houses, but that house was my home. I'd invested twenty-four years in both the inside and the yard to make it the way I wanted it. It was like skin that surrounded my soul. Now I'd agreed to shed my skin.

I'm not sure what Michael had expected me to say, but I didn't believe it was this. We began to strategize about the best way of selling a house in Florida, thousands of miles from our little nest here in Colorado, without making the trip back.

Mingled with the excitement of finally seeing an end to the responsibilities of property and plants (except for my small potted geranium, which I looked at twenty-seven times a day), I felt a virtuous sense of relief. By God, if my hubby contracted Covid-19, it would not be because of anything I'd done or not done. If he had the more precarious health issues, then the decision was more rightly his than mine. Plus, he might well be saving my life with his ultimatum.

Now, if only I could get him to stop going into grocery stores four times a week, to not enter every little shop we walked by, and to refrain from touching every handrail and doorknob he saw, maybe he'd stay healthy.

Meanwhile, I knew I'd be okay. I'd gone through quite a wrestling match coming to a decision. Now I felt relief, and I knew I wouldn't second-guess. It felt right.

CHAPTER II

TAKING CARE OF BUSINESS

We fell in love with Durango. Our RV park was charming and well-maintained, although a bit further out of town than we would've liked. Verizon cell phone service was strong, so I could not complain about weak signals and trouble with internet access. Temperatures dropped to the fifties at night and rose to the upper seventies during the day. Most importantly, with the pandemic mushrooming and the number of Covid-19 cases and deaths soaring each day, we felt safe in this small Rocky Mountain town.

We discovered the eleven-mile Animus River Trail that followed the river through downtown, and we found the Colorado Trail, which went hundreds of miles across the state. We'd walk on the Colorado Trail on weekdays, where the paths were steep, rocky, and narrow. That trail became too crowded on weekends, and we tired of trying to find places to let groups of four adults, seven children, and three dogs pass by.

"How come no one gets off the trail to let us pass?" Michael asked.

"I think because we're too slow. They look at us hobbling along and assume they're faster than we are, which they are."

"But they're coming towards us, not away from us."

I shrugged. He was right. We were the polite ones who always stepped to the side of the trail for others.

Although many of the businesses had closed, Durango had a small, charming downtown area. A few souvenir shops, outdoor clothing retailers, and marijuana dispensaries were open.

"Hey, when did pot dispensaries become essential businesses?" I asked my husband.

"Maybe at the same time DeSantis declared the WWF an essential business. Maybe he set a new standard."

We both laughed. Being from Florida, we paid attention to what Ron DeSantis, the Florida Governor, did. Early on, during the shutdown of essential businesses mandated by the government because of the pandemic, DeSantis dubbed professional fighting and wrestling as an essential business. Yeah, right!

The only thing I didn't like about Durango was the unending wind. Gusts were so strong we didn't dare leave the RV awning out for fear the wind would tear it to shreds. One morning I woke up to find my beautiful and beloved geranium on the gravel, blown off the picnic table by the wind. While the plant suffered only a few broken stems and blooms, the forty-dollar glazed pot had shattered into about a dozen shards. I tried to glue the pieces back together and salvage it, but it didn't work.

My devastation over that geranium accident felt irrational. I realized the plant and pot had been symbolic, a last attempt to hang on to a vestige of my previous lifestyle, the one that had revolved around gardening. Just one beautiful potted plant to look at each day, I'd thought. Although I don't remember the timing exactly, I believe letting go emotionally of that beautiful glazed flower pot helped me let go of everything else in my previous life.

A few days later, I bought a couple of herbs and a larger plastic pot. I made a small dish garden of spearmint, bee balm, and the geranium. While I visualized a beautiful color bowl of my thriller (the geranium, with coral flowers), the filler (the bee balm, with purple flowers), and the spiller (the spearmint), my visualization never materialized. The garden languished, and I soon realized plants that thrived in the Florida humidity were not happy with the constant stress from the strong winds, penetrating sun, and low humidity here in Colorado.

With sadness and relief, I shrugged off my disappointing attempt at a portable garden. Nevertheless, I continued to drag the pathetic dish garden around, looking at it several times a day as I mourned and rejoiced my transformation toward rootlessness. Somehow, that little dish garden now held the only roots I had.

⌂

"Maybe we should call Steve today, see what he thinks about the housing market right now." The day following my promise to sell the house, I felt a sense of urgency to 'do something' before I lost my nerve. Steve and Sandra Vigil, agents at Re/max ACR Elite Group Inc., were our realtor friends in Tampa. They'd just sold one of our rental properties a year earlier. We trusted them.

I'm not sure what all had gone through my head to make me decide to sell. I felt an underlying anxiety every time Michael turned on CNN or listened to David Muir during the ABC News each evening. I had trouble sleeping—I woke up every two or three hours, and sometimes it'd take the same amount of time to fall back asleep. I was often wide awake and up for the day by six A.M.

From what I picked up from the media, I was far from being the only American showing signs of stress. Mental health professionals predicted depression would become the next pandemic. Already, domestic violence and child abuse reports were rising, and people feared the worst as pandemic closures of businesses and schools forced family members to spend inordinate amounts of time together at home. The greatest fears, of which the pundits were not yet addressing, had to do with the economy. What would happen to individual lives with such high unemployment, with the stock market falling, with the food supply interrupted, and with the death toll rising daily from Covid-19?

Despite all the unknowns, I felt happy and safe in Durango. We'd met a couple of full-time RVillagers who worked at the park and another full-time couple across the street from our site. A couple of late afternoon happy hours—outside and 6-ft. apart—had fortified my commitment to becoming a gypsy. I found it reassuring to meet and get to know folks living in their rigs and loving the lifestyle.

"No, there's no need for you to come back to Florida," our realtor friend Steve said. "Folks sell properties from the other side of the country all the time." I'd made the call, and I'd put Steve on speaker phone so that Michael could hear, too.

"Our next-door neighbor has a key. I'll ask him to make a couple of duplicates for you," I said. "Maybe you could go in, look around, and let us know what needs to be done before it's listed. What's happening with the housing market, anyway? Is the middle of a pandemic a good time to try to sell?"

"Prices haven't dropped yet. It's a great time to put your house on the market."

Things moved along quickly. Steve noted a few items that needed attention before he listed the property. Our twenty-two-year-old roof needed replacing, not a surprise but still an expense I'd have been happy not to face. We signed contracts with Steve, a roofing company, an electrician, and a plumber. Steve would supervise the repairs for us. I couldn't believe how quickly and easily everything fell into place.

By the time Steve officially listed the house and put a lockbox on the front door, he'd lined up a lot of buyer interest. Realtors showed the house to about ten prospective buyers in the first two days of the listing, and by the end of the second day, Steve reported four offers, every one at or above the house's list price. The offer we accepted was far above the list price, which more than reimbursed us for the cost of repairs and a new roof.

But how would we empty the house? We sat in lovely Durango, almost two thousand miles from Tampa.

"Michael, I can't do this. How can I let someone go in that house and just haul everything out? There are decisions to make. For God's sake, my mother's ashes are still sitting on the top shelf in the closet in my office. What am I supposed to do? Have someone toss them in the garbage?" I was bordering on hysteria as I considered the mechanics and magnitude of what we were doing.

"Calm down, Little Cherrie," my husband told me. "We can do this. How about contacting Anita next door and see if she'd like to pick up some extra cash by emptying the house for us? She worked at the post office for forty years, and you know how organized and efficient she is."

"Okay, I'll call her today."

Anita accepted the job and proved to be the perfect person for sorting through all our stuff.

If I'd had concerns about going into mourning and becoming depressed over the loss of our roots in Tampa, those concerns proved nonissues. Although I worried that the reality of what we were losing would hit me later, I can say the overwhelming initial feeling was one of relief. It felt liberating to no longer feel the responsibility of home-ownership. I'd never been without owning my own home since I was twenty-five years old, and suddenly I was free.

It was wonderful to have life reduced almost to its lowest common denominator. Things were becoming easier and simpler by the day.

CHAPTER 12

HOW WILL WE GET MAIL?

In Durango, we spent a couple of hours each day on the phone—with our realtor Steve, roofing contractors, plumbers, electricians, and Anita, who was emptying our house. We still had downtime for hiking, socializing with neighbors, and relaxing. I thought I'd also have enough time to do some mail-order shopping.

Michael had had one bad experience already with an online order for face masks. He'd ended up double-charged for masks he never received. Still, we both thought the larger, well-established companies would be reliable, even during a pandemic when online shopping mushroomed in popularity.

We'd been on the road over three months and had brought only a limited supply of clothes with us, mostly winter stuff. Spring had arrived, and we needed shorts and lightweight clothes. Memorial Day weekend online sale prices boggled my mind, with many items more than 60% below regular prices. I pulled out my Visa card and got to work, combing Amazon, Eddie Bauer, and L.L. Bean websites.

Within a couple of hours, I had completed my $300+ clothing order to Eddie Bauer, a one-hundred-year-old business specializing in premium outdoor gear. Michael and I had treated ourselves to a few Eddie Bauer items from our mall store back home in Tampa and loved their products. Why not splurge? The coronavirus had stranded us in God's country here in Colorado, and we needed summer clothes. I ordered two pairs of shorts and a sleeveless blouse for myself and two polo shirts and a sweater for Michael, although I did not understand why Michael thought he needed a sweater for the upcoming summer. Per the online order information, I projected our package would arrive at the RV park in seven to ten days. We planned to be in Durango for another sixteen days. Plenty of time, I'd thought.

I expected our six items of clothing to arrive in one shipment and within the estimated time. But these were not normal times. I first received one pair of shorts in one small plastic bag. A week later, my second pair of shorts arrived. As our check-out date drew closer, I tried to call Eddie Bauer, planning to either cancel the rest of the order or to give new shipping directions.

"I give up," I finally said to Michael. I had tried for several hours on two consecutive days to speak to a real person at Eddie Bauer's. I never made my way through the voicemail maze. "Guess I'll have to ask the park to forward the rest of the order when it comes."

"That should work," Michael said. "They have our credit card on file. We'll just leave it open to pay for the postage until we get our stuff."

I was not pleased to learn the park had a policy of not forwarding mail, which I later realized was standard policy for RV parks. The bottom line on that Memorial Day sale order: it took over two months, but eventually, Eddie Bauer shipped the remaining four items to the Durango RV park, each one individually packaged. We had checked out and moved on long before the packages arrived. The Durango campground systematically marked 'Return to Sender' on each package and handed it back to the mail carrier. Eventually, Eddie Bauer issued a credit to my Visa card.

This Eddie Bauer online order had produced too much stress for my taste, and I decided to wait until stores reopened before adding any more summer clothes to my wardrobe. Anita back in Tampa had boxed up a few items of our clothing and mailed them to us. We could make do with what we had until this pandemic ended, and it became safe to shop in person again.

"This Eddie Bauer experience was a fiasco," I said to Michael. "We've got to get this mail thing figured out. God only knows what kind of important stuff already is sitting at our neighbor's house back home."

"It's not home anymore," my husband pointed out. "Remember?"

When we traveled, Frank, our next-door neighbor in Tampa, collected our mail and notified us if anything looked important. He'd open it, take photographs, and text us the contents. Once the house sold, however, we'd need to have another address.

How do full-time RVers get their mail? This question seemed to be the first one most non-RVers asked when they ran into folks living on the road full-time. (The second most frequently asked question seemed to be what happened to the poop and the pee.) Although we'd already set up almost all our bills for electronic bill payments, there were still some items, like mail-in ballots for voting, that one cannot do electronically. And we'd learned the hard way that it was sometimes difficult to receive packages while on the road.

Before we could set up a mail delivery service, we needed to establish residency. A permanent mailing address was necessary for official business like insurance and registrations on both the car and the RV. It was an election year, and we wanted to vote, which we'd no longer be able to do in Hillsborough County, Florida. Michael booted up his laptop and started exploring our options.

"Hey," he said, "the Florida Division of Highway and Motor Vehicle Safety allows only six weeks for an address change. We also need an address for Medicare, Social Security, our supplemental medical insurance, the Internal Revenue Service, our banks and financial institutions, and voter registration. And, we have to get new drivers' licenses." We looked at each other and sighed. This challenge of so many details at once overwhelmed us.

We knew there were answers to all our questions out there some-where, and we'd talked to enough full-time RVers to realize it didn't take a rocket scientist to figure them out. We dug into the project.

Our new virtual RV community, the Escapees, answered almost all our questions, and we found the additional answers online. We learned there are three popular states for legal residency for full-time RVers: South Dakota, Texas, and Florida. They share the common denomina-tors of no state income taxes and the ease of establishing residency. Had we chosen South Dakota, for example, all we would have needed to do was drive up there, rent a Post Office box, spend one night, and, voila, we'd be South Dakota residents. We could later register the car and RV, transfer the insurance, register to vote, and take care of the other business matters online, on the phone, or through the mail. It now made sense why we'd been seeing so many South Dakota license plates in RV parks for the past four-and-a-half years. Although spending one night in South Dakota made it easy, we had no intention of driving there in the next few weeks. We were quite happy in Colorado.

"We're Florida residents already. It shouldn't be that hard to keep that as our home base," I said. "It'd save a lot of time and hassle."

"But we may not want to return to Florida when we've had enough of RVing."

"So what? I don't see us settling down in Texas or South Dakota either, so what difference does it make?" I asked. "Florida sounds the easiest to me, and besides, we have family and friends there. We'll be going back to Florida for visits if nothing else."

We kept our residency in Florida, and after Michael's painstaking internet research, we chose The Escapees for our mail delivery service. The Escapee's home base for full-time Florida residents was an Escapee-owned RV park in Sumter County. This RV park would be the legal address we'd use for drivers' licenses, car and RV registrations and in-surance, and voter registration. Whenever mail arrived at our Bushnell address, office staff at the park forwarded it to the Escapee Headquarters in Livingston, Texas.

Livingston was the site of the Escapees' official mail forwarding service. The Escapees assigned us a second mailing address for everything that did not pertain to legal, State of Florida business. We'd use this mailing address for things such as banking and investment communications, magazine subscriptions, medical insurance information and statements, and any paper bills, letters, or other U.S. mail. We'd gradually transferred everything possible to electronic notifications and online bill pay over the past few years. The amount of physical mail we received was already low, and we looked forward to no longer receiving junk mail and advertisements. These separate residency and mailing addresses seemed easy and straightforward enough.

We registered to vote in Sumter County, transferred automobile and RV insurance policies to our new Bushnell address, and filled out the Change of Address forms for the automobile and RV registrations quickly and efficiently online. We applied for and received new drivers' licenses within a couple of weeks. Even Medicare and Social Security responded quickly to the change of address requests. It took over three months for financial institutions to answer, with several security layers along the way for each institution.

It was a relief finally to have a reliable, trusted mail forwarding service. The Escapees notified us via email when new mail arrived. I'd then go online, link into our mail forwarding account, and view scanned copies of the envelopes or covers. I could choose whether I wanted the envelopes or magazines destroyed, opened and the inside contents scanned and emailed, or saved and forwarded to us the next time we requested a delivery.

It was easy to have mail forwarded when we stayed in one place for a week or longer. Upon request, the mail forwarding service packed up our mail in a First-Class envelope, and we'd receive it four days later.

When we traveled, it sometimes took a couple of weeks before we could safely request that Escapees forward our mail to either an RV campground or General Delivery at the Post Office in the town where we'd be. (Some RV parks refused to receive mail for their guests.) However, office staff always accepted UPS and FedEx packages. But, just like with those

Eddie Bauer orders that trickled in one item at a time in Durango, RV parks never forwarded mail. If something arrived after we checked out of the park, staff sent it back to the sender.

In the beginning, when I was scared to have an envelope destroyed even when I felt certain it was trash, our monthly mailing fees averaged about $50 per month. As we gradually converted more of our business to paperless electronic delivery, our cost dropped to half that amount. After almost a year on the road, the mail forwarding cost had dropped to about ten bucks a month. We learned never to order items online unless we had a guaranteed delivery date to the campground. Forwarding packages from the mail service in Livingston would sometimes cost as much as the ordered item itself, so we never had packages shipped there.

We grew to appreciate our Amazon Prime account with its free overnight delivery more than ever. As full-time RVers, that $90 annual membership fee paid for itself many times over. And thankfully, deliveries from businesses other than Amazon became more reliable and predictable in time. I've yet to muster the courage to try Eddie Bauer again, but maybe one day . . . (Later, I'd learn I could order my beloved Eddie Bauer clothes from Amazon. Apologies to Eddie Bauer for going through a distributor, and I do feel guilty for expanding Amazon's profits.)

It was a great relief to have our legal affairs in order and a mail forwarding service in place. These were the biggest challenges of transitioning from a stick-and-brick house to life on the road. We patted ourselves on the back for getting it done quickly and efficiently.

CHAPTER 13

CHASING DENNIS HOPPER'S GHOST

Taos looked like a safe place to spend the month of June. We'd spent a week there several years ago and fallen in love with this funky little New Mexico town and the surrounding high desert. It met our criteria of being small (population of 4,700), great weather (average highs of 82 degrees and lows in the mid-forty-degree range), and a low incidence of Covid-19 cases. New Mexico had consistently reported one of the lowest rates of Covid-19 in the United States, and Taos County had lower rates than the State.

We found a very different Taos than the one we'd visited three years earlier. We remembered an artsy, quaint downtown square filled with shops, art galleries, restaurants, and bars. While the businesses were still there, most had 'closed' signs hanging from their locked doors. Our RV park had changed management, and maintenance had taken a nosedive. In the laundry room, for example, only one of the three coin-operated washing machines worked. To make us even more unhappy, management had promised a monthly rate but later refused to honor that verbal agreement. Our month in the park cost more than double what it should have.

Although Taos and Durango were about the same elevation and both were at the lower end of the Rocky Mountains, the difference between forest and desert, and between May and June, made a huge difference in their weather. We'd been physically comfortable in Durango and had even turned the heat on at night a couple of times. Nights in Taos were also chilly, but temperatures soared so high during the afternoons that the air-conditioning rarely cooled the interior below eighty degrees.

While we could not go to restaurants or bars in Taos, Michael latched on to another theme that kept us somewhat occupied for the month. We chased the ghost of Dennis Hopper in what had now become a ghost town itself. It seemed fitting and appropriate.

Dennis Hopper (05/17/1936–05/29/2010) lived in Taos for four tumultuous and turbulent decades. We met and talked with locals who had known Hopper. The last of his five ex-wives continued to live in the area with Hopper's 17-year-old daughter, Galen.

"Oh, God, Michael. Let's watch *Easy Rider* again," I said. "That movie had such a significant impact on me."

"Sure," my accommodating husband said. "I'll pull it up on Netflix." Released in 1969, *Easy Rider* had been the first film actor and filmmaker Dennis Hopper directed. I'd been twenty-one at the time of its debut, and I'd thrilled with the anti-establishment message in the film. Wikipedia indicated no other persona portrayed the 'lost idealism of the 1960s' better than Hopper in this film.

Hopper filmed the hippie commune scenes of *Easy Rider* on location in Taos. While shooting the movie, he reportedly fell in love with the area and purchased a house in 1970. Our retracing of Hopper's steps and legacy began with a trip to the Mabel Dodge Luhan House, Hopper's first Taos home. It was a huge, sprawling, abandoned-looking property that until recently had been open to the public for tours. We later learned the property now serves as an inn for artist retreats and workshops.

"I can't believe it's closed." Michael almost wailed in disappointment. "I really wanted to see the inside."

"Looks like peeking in the windows is as close as you're going to get," I said. And peek in the windows we did. The house appeared fully furnished as if whoever lived there would be back in time for dinner. We saw no signs of life inside.

We weren't the only ones at the property. We chatted briefly to a young couple eating take-out lunches on an outside picnic table, and we saw an older man who, like us, was peeking through the dark panes trying to see what was inside.

Michael had talked with enough locals and done enough internet research to have stories to share with these fellow interlopers. "Hopper married his fourth wife in this place, and the wedding party lasted eight days," he said to the young couple. "The party and the marriage ended at the same time." Everybody laughed.

"Jeez," I moaned. "I sure wish I could see the doors to those kitchen cabinets." Local sources had told us Georgia O'Keefe had painted flowers on the cabinet doors, a bit of trivia that seemed consistent with the heavily padlocked doors to the house but inconsistent with the lack of external security. But then, maybe there were hidden security cameras and burglar alarms connected to local law enforcement stations.

Michael had yet another Hopper party story he liked to tell. "His parties used to go on for days. I read that Hopper once stumbled into the dining room and found about twenty people there, all making themselves at home. He didn't recognize a single one of them and kicked them all out," Michael said. "This place had some hell of debauchery going on."

During the 1970s and 1980s, Hopper had a reputation as one of Hollywood's most notorious drug and alcohol addicts. Wikipedia reports that at his peak, Hopper ingested up to three grams of cocaine a day. A local trolley tour guide we'd met in Taos in 2017 told a story we still remembered. "I used to see Hopper in the mornings here in the town square," the guide had said. "He always had a coffee cup with him as he walked around, taking sips from time to time." Our guide had laughed. "No one ever believed Hopper had coffee in that mug." During this period of addiction and wild parties, the town scorned Hopper and had little to do with him. Wikipedia described him as an "outcast."

Hopper redeemed himself in the eyes of the townsfolks when his movies *Hoosiers* and *Blue Velvet* became blockbusters. While I could not determine whether he ever stopped drinking and drugging, he nevertheless further won the locals' acceptance when he sold the Mabel Dodge Luhan House and his outrageous parties came to a halt.

Doctors diagnosed Hopper with prostate cancer in 2008. His cancer metastasized to his bones, and he passed away in 2010, shortly after his seventy-fourth birthday.

"Let's go see the church again where his funeral was held," I said to Michael.

"Yes! And then I want to find his grave. The cemetery where he's buried is about a mile down the road and is called the Jesus Nazareno Cemetery."

We had visited the San Francisco de Asis Mission Church in 2017 on our last Taos visit. Located in Ranchos de Taos, the small, one-roomed adobe structure was less than two miles from our RV park. The last time we were there, workers had been resurfacing the adobe walls, and we encountered lots of activity and construction. While there was no construction going on during this visit, someone had locked the double-front doors, so we weren't able to peek inside, as we'd done previously.

"Jeez," I said. "Are you sure he's buried in this place?" We'd driven west from the church, found the dirt road turnoff for the cemetery, and bounced down a one-laned pig trail to find a small cemetery behind some vacant buildings. "Wow, many of these graves don't even have stones, just little wooden crosses or hand-painted plaques with names and dates. Why would Dennis Hopper have chosen to be buried in this place?"

"He loved Taos, felt connected to the people here," Michael said.

The day was hot, and we both sweated under the intense desert sun. We wandered through the weeds, wildflowers, and barely-marked graves for at least half an hour, unable to find Hopper's marker.

"I mean, surely he has a gravestone, don't you think?" I asked.

"Hey, keep it down. I think I'm channeling Dennis Hopper," my husband said.

We gave up and left the cemetery without finding Hopper's grave. A couple of days later, after asking around in town, Michael received directions from a local, and we finally found Hopper's final resting site.

"How the hell could we have missed this?" I asked. "If it'd been a rattlesnake, we would've been bitten."

Someone had marked Hopper's grave with a large hand-hewn wooden cross, consistent with so many other primitive-looking markers. Weeds grew on the ground above his casket, just as they did on most other plots. But Hopper's grave was an eye-catcher, unlike the others. Visitors had paid tribute to Hopper's life and legacy by tying bandanas on the cross's arms. Neither of us could believe we hadn't spotted the site immediately on our first cemetery trip.

In our RV park in Taos, we met and became friends with two couples from Riverside, California—Craig and Arline Bringhurst and Bill and Diane Wolff. We later learned that they, too, had tracked down Hopper's grave in Taos. And like us, they also had a lot of trouble finding the grave.

Craig, with typical humor, referred to the entire cemetery as "home-made." How fittingly that word described all those makeshift, cobbled together, individually designed grave-sites. I don't remember a single headstone that looked like it came from a professional engraver at a tombstone business. It was shocking to realize that the great Dennis Hopper's gravesite looked as humble as all the others. It almost made me want to buy something to show him proper respect, even if he'd never know I'd done it.

Michael took many photos. Hopper's story had captured my husband's heart and attention, and he continued with his lighthearted theme of 'channeling' Dennis Hopper. It seemed to fit.

Taos was like a ghost town. Other than tracking down Dennis Hopper sites and stories, we did little in Taos other than finish up the business of selling our house in Tampa, take hikes in the desert and Carson National Forest, and enjoy socially-distanced happy hours in the RV park with our new friends from Riverside, California. During our previous Taos visit, we'd eaten in restaurants, drank in bars, visited ski resorts, and attended a local open mic where I'd read an excerpt from my first book. We'd also toured The Greater World Earthship Community, the country's largest community of autonomous, eco-friendly, sustainable, off-the-grid houses made from recycled materials. I would have loved to see all those Earthships again, but our fear of Covid-19 kept us away. It's just another 'next time' thing to do, I thought. Surely this pandemic will end soon.

It felt as though Dennis Hopper's ghost still lived in Taos—I felt the vibes just as my husband did. We concluded that Taos was a ghost town in more ways than one.

During our month in Taos, Michael and I spent several hours each week on speaker phone with Anita, our next-door neighbor back home. Anita touched every item in our house as we decided what to put in the garbage, give to my daughter Kate, give to friends and neighbors, sell, have shipped to us, and put into storage for a future when we would settle down again. At the end of three weeks, we had whittled our possessions down to just enough stuff to fill one 10' X 12' storage bin at Cube Smart. Plus, we'd made many of our friends and neighbors happy with the bounty, anything from our lanai steel-tipped darts and bristle board, to gardening supplies galore, to outdoor furniture and garden art, to potted plants, to an elliptical trainer. Knowing that furniture would deteriorate in storage over time, we sold or gave away almost all the inside furnishings.

There were two times during the emptying of our home of the past twenty-three years when I broke down and cried. The first was when so many of my mother's treasures, such as her bronzed baby shoes and an antique picture of her as a baby with her mother, went into the garbage. No, I did not throw away her ashes that had sat for almost fifteen years on the top shelf of a closet. I convinced my daughter to keep them for me. Eventually, I'd figure out an appropriate way to honor them.

Tears came a second time when Anita started emptying the gardening shed at the end of the house. My neighbors had a field day, dividing up all the containers, supplies, and tools that had brought me so much pleasure and satisfaction through the years. While happy that these things were going to friends who appreciated them, it still stung, especially to know that some of my accumulated gardening treasures had come from my mother's gardening shed. I wondered if I'd ever recover from the losses of both my mother and my gardening.

The closing on the house was so uneventful as to be forgettable. We notarized our signatures on all the documents and FedExed them to the title company five days before the official closing. Everything went without a hitch. I do not even remember what we did on the day of the closing. I clearly remember, however, driving for over an hour to a Bank of America branch in Santa Fe to secure the wire transfer of the proceeds from the sale. We resisted withdrawing a single penny of the money—we would save it for our next sticks-and-bricks home when the time came that we could no longer manage an RV.

Another closed chapter, and finally, Michael had what he'd dreamed of for over four years of RV travel. We were official, full-time RVers at last.

Our house and life back in Tampa quickly faded into ghost-like memories, ephemeral shapes of the past that grew hazier and more distant by the day. I wondered if down the road I'd ever try to track down those ghosts. Maybe I could find and channel my mother like Michael had found and channeled Dennis Hopper. The thought made me smile.

CHAPTER 14

KOI FISHING IN CRIPPLE CREEK

We booked a month in Cripple Creek, Colorado, looking for cool summer temperatures, good hiking trails, and few cases of Covid-19. It seemed like a safe place for a couple of old folks like us to bide time.

The town of Cripple Creek sat at a 9,494-ft. elevation and had fewer than 1,500 residents. It was the county seat of Teller County, which had a population of around 25,000. Doctors had diagnosed only eighty cases of Covid-19 in the entire county, seventy-nine of which had been resolved. Michael obsessed about what 'resolved' meant in Colorado.

"Does it mean they took those infected people out and shot them?" he asked with a laugh. Besides that lingering, unanswered question of possible death from a firing squad, we didn't think we could have found a safer place to hang out for a month.

We'd been on the road over five months, and every new month had brought new restrictions and mandates governing public places. It had gotten to the point we didn't even feel safe going into a grocery store or a pharmacy, although we continued to do both. We hoped a month in this isolated mountain village would help us feel safe again, even if the world no longer felt that way.

Our RV park, two blocks from the main drag, would be our Cripple Creek home for the month of July and the first week in August. The park was a small, seedy place filled chiefly with full-timers who seemed to either work in the hospitality industry downtown or not work at all. When other forms of amusement eluded us, Michael and I would sit in the RV, watch our neighbors through our one-way tinted windows, and make up funny stories about their lives. We named one small, wiry, hyperactive guy 'Rip.' With his chest-length Colorado beard and ragged clothing, he reminded me of the Rip Van Winkle rendering in Washington Irving's short story by that name.

We had fun speculating about a couple of hippies who lived in a pop-art RV not far from our rig. The woman appeared to have a day job somewhere nearby, but the guy stayed home and seemed to constantly slap a new coat of paint somewhere on the exterior of their older Class C motorhome. He used bright, tropical colors and created abstract designs.

Out of curiosity, Michael asked the park manager about the eye-catching rig. "Oh, that guy's an artist," the manager said. "He usually leaves in the summer, drives the rig all over Colorado to these children's art camps. He lets the kids paint on the thing, too. Couldn't do it this year because of the coronavirus."

I, too, had a question for that guy in the office, and his answer didn't please me. It was about the small ladies' room in the park. Although we had used our RV black tank for what the good Lord intended, Michael and I both used campground bathhouses once a day if they appeared clean, sanitized, and empty of other users. These were important criteria for us during this time of Covid-19. I'd argued with my stubborn husband that it was insane to use a public bathroom during the pandemic unless we had no alternative. However, as he is wont to do, my persuasive husband convinced me that an empty bathhouse with adequate ventilation and cleanliness would be preferable to risking tank problems in our rig.

Our RV park was old, and I'm guessing no one had updated the electrical and plumbing in the bathhouses for decades. When I first went into the ladies' room and flipped on the light switch, only one of the four fluorescent light bulbs in the two overhead fixtures came on. "What the hell?" I asked. I had to leave the door cracked even to have enough light to find my way to the stall.

I dealt with this dark ladies' room for about a week before deciding to take it up with management.

"What's with all the burned-out light bulbs in the ladies' room?" I asked the manager. "Are there plans to replace them anytime soon?"

"Nope." We'd come to understand that locals in these small mountain towns didn't waste words. "Fixtures are out of date. They no longer make bulbs for 'em."

We stared at each other for a while. "Well, are there any plans to replace the fixtures? It's pretty dark in there."

The manager shrugged. "Up to the owner," he said. "No idea what he plans to do."

What could I say? Absolutely nothing. If I didn't like a dark bathroom and if I minded leaving the door cracked, I supposed I could use the toilet in my rig. Remembering my husband's persuasive argument that a public restroom was safe if there was adequate ventilation, I realized a cracked door contributed to better air circulation. Should I feel relieved about the burnt-out light bulbs? I sighed.

We had chosen this RV park because it was only two blocks from Bennett Avenue, the main street in town. What a surprise when we walked uptown the first time. Michael had neglected to tell me gambling had replaced gold-mining as Cripple Creek's major source of revenue.

"Michael!" I almost shouted with excitement. "I can go Koi fishing! Surely one of these casinos has a Koi pond."

"Are you crazy? You can't go in a friggin' casino. We're in the middle of a pandemic. You trying to kill yourself?"

I knew my husband was right. It would be suicidal to walk into a casino, especially after some of the stories we'd already heard from locals. The Fourth of July weekend had just ended, and the streets had teemed with tourists coming up on tour buses from Colorado Springs, a couple of hours away. The reason for the deluge of casino goers was easy to understand. A week before the Fourth of July weekend, the Governor of Colorado had ordered all bars to shut down. However, the state allowed casinos to stay open, and casinos were places where alcohol flowed freely. Having arrived on tour buses, these revelers could drink themselves silly without risking an arrest for drinking and driving.

The casinos had strict safety protocols—a temperature check at the entrance, mandated masks, social distancing, and only 50% of guest capacity. Casino managements had tried to enforce the requirements. They didn't want citations, or worse yet, to have the State close them down.

The holiday weekend had not gone as management had hoped. Employees described the guests as so starved for a good party that once inside the casino, they discarded their masks, crowded three-deep at the bars, and drank themselves into oblivion. The town was almost holding its collective breath to see if Covid-19 cases would spike following the Independence Day weekend. Later we heard that infections among locals had not risen, perhaps because the employees always wore masks. We never learned whether all those guzzling gamblers infected each other and took the virus back home to their families and friends.

These were not stories Michael and I wanted to hear. We'd come to Cripple Creek to feel safe. Worrying about a coronavirus uptick and getting sick ourselves was not on our agenda.

Cripple Creek was the site of the greatest mining boom in Colorado history. Miners began arriving in the 1890s, and the boom lasted until after World War II. The town sat in a large valley at the base of Pike's Peak. Many of the surrounding mountains reflected the ravages of strip mining, with nothing left but huge barren mounds of clay, rocks, and boulders.

Michael and I loved walking up and down the hilly streets in town. We fantasized about living in one of the stately old Victorian-style two and three-story houses. Many had sheer lace curtains in the windows, rocking chairs on the front porches, and flower-filled window boxes attached to the railings. I imagined all my stresses and problems melting away if I lived in a place like this.

Cripple Creek was sufficiently small that we began to feel like we knew some of the residents. We talked to a waiter at the Pint and Platter, an Irish pub casino on the main street, several times on the sidewalk as he took smoke breaks. The post office was so small it had only two employees and no mail delivery to street addresses. Townsfolk had to rent boxes and collect their mail in-person. We received our forwarded mail via General Delivery to the post office. After our first pick-up, the post-mistress said, "You don't have to bring in your drivers' licenses anymore. I know who you are now."

During his early twenties, Michael lived in Woodland Park, Colorado, about thirty miles from Cripple Creek. He'd worked in a gold mine in Victor, ten miles south of Cripple Creek. He loved being back in the area and talking to locals, many of whom had worked or still worked in the mining industry. Many of the mines had closed in recent years, and we spoke with a fair number of angry, bitter unemployed miners. They hated Obama for having tightened environmental regulations, which put many of the smaller mines out of business. What a dilemma. How can a country protect the environment and still extract essential minerals to keep the economy moving forward?

"It's not just the strip mining," one retired miner pointed out. "All mining destroys the environment. What the hell are we supposed to do? The country wants its goddamn gold, but then it passes laws to make it impossible for us to mine it."

We felt the angst of these struggling ex-miners. It was yet another example of a complex issue with no clear answers.

⌂

I never tried to count the number of casinos in Cripple Creek, but I watched with interest as the tour buses pulled up and dropped off their passengers. I couldn't believe how many older folks came from Colorado Springs to gamble. Bus drivers had to help many of the passengers down the steps. We watched drivers pull canes, walkers, and wheelchairs from bus basements, then steady each passenger on the sidewalk before moving on to assist the next one. I saw folks with nasal cannulas pulling wheeled oxygen tanks behind them. I saw one elderly man rush out of a casino with urine running down his pants legs. I wondered why these older adults, already compromised with medical issues, would risk going into a casino during a pandemic.

But maybe I shouldn't act so surprised. I don't remember when or where I first played a slot machine, but as I'd aged, the appeal had increased. Exponentially after I'd discovered a Koi slot machine game at the Gold Dust West Casino in Reno, Nevada, a couple of years earlier.

I'd seen slot machines with Koi games in quite a few casinos. The games had names such as the Lucky Koi, the Pond of Koi, Koi Garden, and others. Most were quiet and tried to capture the serene, calm of a Japanese water garden. However, the one I discovered and fell in love with in Reno was anything but quiet. My Koi slot machine, called Fate of the 8 Power Wheel, was noisy and chaotic, characterized by sirens, bells, whistles, clangs, and more. When one spun a giant wheel and the arrow hit the number eight, a huge screen appeared with Koi swimming around on a background of water. To earn points, one had to touch the Koi. The more Koi one touched, the more points one won.

I recently watched a YouTube video of a guy playing Fate of the 8 Power Wheel. He sat calmly on the stool in front of the big screen, gently poking Koi fish with the index finger on his right hand.

"What the hell, Michael? You've got to come watch this." I couldn't believe what I saw, and neither could Michael.

"Wow. Bet he doesn't accumulate many points or win many free games. Shame you can't show him how to fish," Michael said.

We walked up and down Bennett Avenue more times than I could count during our month in Cripple Creek. Every time we passed a casino entrance, I thought of how much fun I'd had in Reno fishing for Koi. When the bells rang and the whistles blew, I'd jump to my feet and start slapping the screen as fast and hard as I could with two open palms. I'd yell and scream, cheer and call for Michael to come to watch. I won lots of money and free games fishing for Koi. I'd give almost anything to do it again.

This pandemic had turned our lives upside down. Although I still felt the excitement of my new freedom from the responsibilities of home-ownership, the reality of these current restrictions hit me hard.

What an oxymoron. In some ways, I was freer than I'd ever been in my life, but in other ways, I'd had most of my liberties removed. I could no longer go in and out of buildings without a mask, and I didn't go into any buildings unless necessary. I could no longer eat in restaurants, socialize with friends, even pay airfare to bring my daughter out west for a visit. Anything other than staying home, hiking on a trail, or sitting in the car felt risky.

Michael was right. No matter how much I wanted to do it or how much fun it would be, I could not go fishing for Koi in a casino in Cripple Creek, Colorado.

I only hoped I could maintain the necessary self-discipline to live through this horror that had become my world. I empathized with all those elderly folks easing down the tour bus steps, waiting for the drivers to retrieve their mobility aids so they could make their way into these casinos. Maybe they'd find Fate of the Power 8 Wheel, and maybe, just maybe, they'd have as much fun fishing for Koi as I'd had.

I understood why folks in this country refused to comply with the Center for Disease Control's (CDC) coronavirus recommendations to stay home, wear a mask when outside, and maintain at least six feet between people. I felt like a kid throwing a temper tantrum, but I wanted my life back. The old one. The one in which I could've walked into that damned casino and spent three hours slapping my hands against a screen, trying to smack Koi.

If I ever return to Cripple Creek and a casino still stands on Bennett Avenue, I vow to march right in and fish even if the pandemic is still in full force. I wouldn't care that the fish weren't alive and the water wasn't wet. But for now, I must live with the unrequited dream of Koi fishing in Cripple Creek.

CHAPTER 15

WIKING IN LEADVILLE

It was with both disappointment and relief to find that Leadville, Colorado, our next small-town stay, did not have casinos. If it had, I'm sure I would have gotten myself in trouble. I could only hope that our new RV park, one block from the main street, would offer us some places to walk and maybe even a restaurant with outside seating for an occasional mid-afternoon happy hour.

Michael and I developed agreed-upon pandemic rules for ourselves. We wouldn't go inside a bar or restaurant, and we'd consider outside seating only when the tables were well-spaced. We would go into only grocery and drug stores, and we'd try to plan better to minimize the number of trips.

Concerns about our safety fluctuated in direct proportion to spikes in the number of Covid-19 cases, and for the most part, cases increased rather than decreased. We wanted to live, and we knew we had to assume responsibility for our health. We also understood the need to work together. It made no sense for one of us to take more risks than the other. If one of us got sick, the other most certainly would. RVs didn't lend themselves to indoor social distancing.

We arrived in Leadville in early August 2020. With an elevation of 10,152-ft. (the highest incorporated municipality in the United States), the area promised comfortable weather both day and night. Sitting in the middle of the San Isabel National Forest in the heart of the Rocky Mountains and near the Colorado River's headwaters, the area was a mecca for hikers, fishermen, rock climbers, boaters, hunters, campers, and outdoor lovers of every ilk. Combine these facts with a population of under 3,000 permanent residents and a low incidence of Covid-19. Michael and I thought we'd found Nirvana.

Leadville is also where we discovered the 'wike.'

Like Cripple Creek, Leadville had been a significant mining town back in the mid-nineteenth century. The boom began when miners discovered gold during the Pikes Peak Gold Rush in the late 1850s. But the gold was difficult to mine because of black, slushy, sandy sediments. Frustration turned to excitement when assay-conducted tests identified those sediments as cerussite, a mineral with a high silver content. While Cripple Creek became a gold mining capitol, Leadville mushroomed into one of the world's largest and richest silver camps.

Harrison Avenue, Leadville's main street, was about the same length as Bennett Avenue in Cripple Creek. But instead of casinos, Leadville had gift shops, restaurants and coffee shops, and more bars than I could count. We found an occasional thrift store, dentist's office, and beauty salon squeezed in among the businesses that catered to tourists.

Unlike Cripple Creek, which hosted no dispensaries, Leadville had several. The State of Colorado had legalized recreational marijuana in 2012. There were laws against consuming marijuana in public places, and we never saw anyone smoking a joint on the sidewalk. However, our noses told us folks were taking calculated risks and bending those rules.

We'd planned to stay in Leadville through Labor Day, usually the last of the prominent tourist weekends. While July and August were peak tourist times for these outdoor meccas in the mountains, we never felt crowded or at risk. Everyone seemed to take mask-wearing and social distancing seriously, and we were grateful. However, when we'd peek in open doors of barrooms during our daily walks, I'd gaze with longing at those barstools. We shook our heads, imagining what it'd be like to sit in an old saloon established in the mid-1800s.

We talked with a couple of dedicated hikers at one of Leadville's sidewalk cafes one afternoon during happy hour. To celebrate making it to the top of yet another fourteen-thousand-foot mountain, they had hit all the Leadville bars the previous evening.

"How were they?" Michael asked. "Were they crowded?"

One of the guys laughed. "Well, except for a couple of snockered locals here and there, we talked to a lot of bored, idle bartenders."

One of these days, we vowed to return and drink ourselves silly in one of those quaint old establishments. I could hardly wait.

"My God, Michael," I said. "I friggin' can't believe the view out our front window." Michael had just stumbled from the bedroom at 8:30 A.M., and I sat perched in the passenger seat in my RV office. "Come look at Mount Elbert. There was more snow last night."

Despite being half asleep, Michael stumbled over to look. "Wow," he muttered as he turned back towards the kitchen to pour a cup of coffee. I'd been up almost three hours already, writing. Early mornings were my most productive and favorite time to write.

"You know, I cannot imagine ever in my life finding a more beautiful view out our front windshield. It's just incredible. I could stay here forever." Our Leadville RV park was tiny, cramped, old, and ugly. However, from my office perch I enjoyed a dead-on view of Mount Elbert, Colorado's highest peak (14,440-ft.) and the second-highest peak in the contiguous United States (the highest is Mount Whitney which is 14,505-ft. and sits in the Sierra Nevada Mountains of California). I'd always assumed Pikes Peak was Colorado's tallest since that seemed to be the most popular of all the peaks. When I looked it up on the internet, it surprised me to learn Pikes Peak was only 14,115-ft.

Combine the awesome view of Mount Elbert with the charm of downtown Leadville, and I felt like I'd landed in God's Country for sure. We'd found a couple of places with outside seating and great wings. We even considered crowding into a rooftop patio that featured live happy hour music in addition to drinks and wings, but luckily, our better judgments prevailed. We'd found wonderful places to hike on the Colorado Trail, at the Leadville National Fish Hatchery's Nature Trail, and on trails along Turquoise Lake. We were both so enamored with Leadville that Michael was lobbying hard that we should see a realtor and sign a six-month lease to spend the winter there.

"Just think," my excited husband said. Repeatedly. "A little cabin, six cords of wood, a wood-burning stove, and a satellite dish. We'd be so safe and snug."

"It gets forty degrees below zero here," I said. "You've lost your friggin' mind."

"I've lived in Colorado. You don't understand. While it drops down below zero at night, the minute the sun comes up the next morning, the temperatures rise. You'd be comfortable outside in short sleeves by ten o'clock in the morning, even if there were four feet of snow on the ground."

"Dream on, husband of mine. I'm not doing it."

However, to placate him, I agreed to stop in at a realtor's office to inquire about rentals. "No one around here gives a six-month lease," the realtor had said. "You'd have to commit for a year."

"Glad that's settled," I said as we left the office. "We don't have to talk about this again, right?"

However, discussions about cold weather were not over, and I'm happy to report that my sweet hubby could become as freaked about cold weather as I could. We were Floridians, after all.

We found our stride in Leadville and committed to walking/hiking four to six days a week. The weather was great, the trails were gorgeous, and social isolation was easy. We might have even done more had it not been for my degenerated arthritic feet and Michael's poor balance and chronic pain from his poorly healed shoulder. With the regular exercise, fresh air, and sunshine, we slept like babies at night. Our stamina improved, we both noticed a welcomed weight loss of several pounds, and we felt more physically fit than we'd felt in years.

And, it was in Leadville that we discovered the 'wike.'

"Huh?" I asked. "Say that again."

"That woman wished us a 'good wike,' Michael said.

"What are you talking about?"

"That woman on the trail, the one we just passed. She wished us a good wike. I might have heard wrong, but I don't think so." Michael stopped and waited for me to catch up. "Or maybe she just accidentally said 'wike' rather than 'hike.' But I like it. A lot. It's like a little more than a walk but maybe not strenuous enough to be a hike. That's sort of what we do. We wike."

"It's not even a 'sort of,'" I said. "That's exactly what we do." And thus, we began our Facebook posts about our wikes, which brought chuckles and smiles to our friends back in Tampa.

We had realized in Taos in May that our RV propane furnace didn't work. It would come on for fifteen seconds, blow cold air, and then shut off. "No problem," Michael said. "This is summer. We have an appointment for our warranty repairs and routine service in mid-September in Colorado Springs. We won't need heat before then."

We'd never RVed at such a high elevation as Leadville, and temps routinely sank into the low 50s to upper 40s at night. We bought a small electric space heater to use when temperatures dropped. At first, we were nervous about going to sleep with a space heater running. We changed our minds in double-time when we woke up one morning to find the outside temperature at thirty-nine degrees and the inside at forty-nine. We rushed to Leadville's small ACE hardware store and bought a second heater.

Both our space heaters had low and high settings. The low settings ran at 750 watts and the high at 1500 watts. We quickly learned that running both heaters at high settings tripped the circuit breaker. We compromised and ran only one heater on high overnight, then turned on both heaters in the mornings at low settings.

I later learned that we should have plugged the heaters into GFCI breakers or surge protectors to prevent the entire electrical system in our motorhome from going poof. I also learned that a heater and a coffee pot turned on at the same time would trip the surge protector. It became tricky to manage heaters in a rig that had only two GFCI breakers and enjoy morning coffee at the same time.

Even with the space heater running all night on high, I would often get up at 6:00 or 6:30 A.M. and find inside temperatures in the low to mid-fifties. "I'm going to be a true Colorado girl before I leave here," I said to Michael one morning. "I'm toughening up."

In fairness, though, fifty-three degrees with 21% humidity felt a lot more comfortable than a Florida fifty-three-degree temperature with 87% humidity. Maybe I wasn't so tough after all.

I especially felt like a wimp when we learned that the young couple camping next to us, Jacob and Stephanie, had moved into this Leadville RV park the previous February and had slept in a small tour bus with no heat at all. They worked in the entertainment industry, Jacob as a maintenance worker in a large hotel in Vail and Stephanie as a server in Breckenridge. We saw them both outside in t-shirts, shorts, and flip-flops on those thirty-nine-degree mornings. Maybe I'd never become a true Colorado girl. I knew sleeping without heat and running around in flip-flops were not in my immediate future.

As August ended and September arrived, we could feel and smell a touch of fall in the air. The young aspen saplings began to turn yellow, and the daytime temperatures stayed in the seventies rather than rising to the low eighties. We had a couple of rainy days in which the temperature never broke seventy degrees. Perfect, in our opinion. We had grown to love these cooler temps. (Except at night, when I would get cold.)

Then the weather shifted, bringing a cold arctic blast from the north our way. When meteorologists in Colorado Springs predicted that the temperature in Leadville could drop as low as nine degrees with up to 6-in. of snow, we quickly decided it was time to taking our wiking down to a lower elevation. The problem was that the worst of the weather would come over the Labor Day weekend. How would we ever find a reservation in an RV park in Colorado during the last major camping weekend of the year?

I reached a couple of new insights about myself during our Leadville stay. First, I realized that I would never be a Colorado girl in terms of coping with cold weather. Maybe my Southern blood was just too thin. Second, I understood that no matter how hard I tried or how much I wanted it, I'd never progress to the point of hiking. I could only hope to maintain my newly-claimed status as a wiker rather than a walker with my arthritic feet. While these new realizations saddened me, they also increased my determination to keep on moving with this RVing. We needed to keep going as long as we possibly could.

Our adoption of the term wiking triggered a marching musical mantra for me. Enter Nancy Sinatra. During our final wikes in Leadville, before heading down to a lower, hopefully warmer, elevation, 'these boots are made for wiking' rhythmically looped through my mind with every step.

CHAPTER 16

MORE REASONS TO RUN

Running from Covid-19 is one thing. Running from snow is something altogether different. I didn't like running from either.

Folks in Leadville had never seen snow this early in the year. Even Colorado Springs, at a much lower elevation of only 6,030-ft., would get a few inches of snow. Folks in our little Leadville RV park started packing to leave as soon as they heard the forecast. We began preparing, too, mainly since our furnace didn't work. It had already dropped as low as forty-nine degrees in the rig at night with two space heaters running. I could not imagine how low the inside might dip if the outside temps dropped to nine degrees on Labor Day.

We had not winterized our rig and hadn't a clue how to go about doing it. Folks had warned us that thousands of dollars of damage could occur if pipes and tanks froze and burst. We could not risk damaging our motorcoach. It was now the only place we could call home.

Michael got on both his iPad and his phone. He even searched on Google Chrome for an RV park further south with an available site. I say 'even' because ordinarily, he would have relied solely on his beloved AllStays RV & Campground app to find us a place to stay. Although he would never admit it, I sensed he felt as anxious as I did over our situation. I didn't think I'd fare much better in nine-degree weather than would our rig.

The next couple of days were tense. Finally, on Saturday afternoon Michael found an RV park in Green Mountain Falls that promised to put us up somewhere in the park. However, it might be Tuesday, September 8th, before the manager could guarantee full hookups. Still, the park was a couple of thousand feet down the mountains from Leadville, and the prediction for the night in Green Mountain Falls was a low of only twenty degrees. Not perfect, but better than nine degrees. Michael snapped up the offer.

We arrived at the RV park in Green Mountain Falls on Sunday afternoon, September 6th. Our car thermometer read ninety degrees for the outside temperature. Management placed us overnight in its RV storage lot, where we would boondock until a space became available in the campground. Once we leveled the rig, opened the slides, and turned on the generator to run the air-conditioning, we took off in the car to explore.

"I'm so hot," I said. "It's just friggin' unbelievable to think tomorrow night the temperature will drop to twenty degrees and snow will fall."

"Yeah, I know," Michael said. "But look, the temperature is already dropping." He laughed as he pointed to the car thermometer. It had fallen all the way from ninety degrees down to eighty-nine.

We found The Blue Moose, a charming outdoor café in Green Mountain Falls, where we drank beer, ate wings, and listened to an acoustic musician. In the outside patio's shade, the temperature was comfortable, with the thermometer dropping as the sun dipped behind the mountains. It was a great way to end a day that'd already been far too stressful, especially with the mass exodus of cars, trucks, and RVs trying to get to more hospitable locations further south before the storm arrived.

Although not experienced boondockers, we had no apprehensions about spending the night without hookups in the park's storage lot. We just felt relieved to have found refuge from the pending storm. Our relief was such that I don't think either of us worried that this would be the first time we'd camped in the snow.

We were lucky. Campers were evacuating the park where we were waiting to get in, and by noon on Labor Day, management had assigned us a beautiful, premier site at the top of the hill on a paved pad looking out at mountains in the distance and the park below. We had time to get set up and situated, run into town for last-minute supplies, and take stock. Weather predictions were getting worse—lower temperatures, more snow, and a longer duration for the cold snap.

Michael went into emergency mode. A low of twenty-six degrees had been one thing, but predictions for temperatures in the teens were more than we could face in an RV with no heat other than a couple of small space heaters. Again, we got lucky. A mobile RV service out of Colorado Springs agreed to drive up to Green Mountain Falls and look at our furnace. We yelled and cheered with relief, neither asking nor caring how much it would cost.

Our still-under-warranty furnace remains an enigma. The mobile mechanic, Ron, looked around at the furnace, jiggled a few things, and the furnace sprang to life. He shrugged his shoulders. "I have no idea why it stopped working or why it suddenly started," he said. "My best guess would be that maybe some wires jiggled loose when you hit a bump, and I wiggled them just right, so now they're making contact again."

"Do you think it's going to keep working?" I was afraid to ask but did. "It's going to get very cold."

"Wish I could promise you it will, but I don't know." Ron recommended we keep the thermostat down as low as we could stand it to reduce the likelihood of it shutting off again.

Ron freaked out when we told him we'd been running two electric space heaters off the motorhome's electrical system. "Oh, no," he'd said with a groan.

"Yeah, we sort of knew it was dangerous, but now we're plugging them into either a GFCI plug or one of our surge protectors," I said.

"Still not good," Ron said. "What you've been doing is very, very dangerous. Be glad you haven't destroyed your rig." He told us to get a 30-amp to 110-volt converter and plug an extension cord into the converter on the 30-amp post at our site. We could then run the extension cord through a window, which would create a draft but was a minor price to pay compared to the consequences of destroying the entire electrical system. With a surge protector plugged into the extension cord, we could safely run our two space heaters.

I suppose Ron had no trouble figuring out that we knew nothing about cold weather RVing. He lingered after our furnace arose from the dead and 'gently' walked us through all the necessary procedures to prepare for the storm. We needed to drain all the tanks, including the water heater, and any water that might remain in the pipes and drains. I say Ron did this 'gently' because he somehow explained it without making us feel like total idiots. I cringe to consider the damage that might have resulted to our motorhome had this mobile RV mechanic not coached us through these things we would never have otherwise known to do.

"Jeez," I later said to Michael. "How the hell are people supposed to know things like this?"

My husband only shrugged and rolled his eyes.

The almost $300 trip fee and service charge for the furnace repair were worth every penny. For the first few hours after Ron left, we held our breath every time the furnace kicked off and cheered every time it kicked back on. It continued to work properly, although we both wanted like hell to push the thermostat up to about seventy-eight. Instead, we kept it around sixty-six. The Colorado temperatures remained below freezing for three days, and even with our two space heaters running almost constantly, our indoor temperature never rose above sixty-three degrees.

A Facebook friend informed me that God had built Interstate 10 as a warning that one should never go north of that Interstate after September 1st. I vowed to pay attention to my friend's advice in the future.

"You know," I said to Michael on the second day of hibernation inside the rig, "if we ever get caught like this again with a freaky arctic blast heading right towards us, I don't care if we have to drive forty-eight consecutive hours to out-run it. I don't ever want to be this cold for this long again!"

"You can't mean that," my husband said. "Remember how miserable we both get when it gets up in the upper eighties and nineties? This hasn't been nearly as bad as being too hot."

"I disagree, and I don't care how beautiful and magical and fairyland-like this friggin' snow might be. I'm cold."

I meant it. While Colorado remains one of my favorite places in the entire Universe, RVing in the snow makes no sense whatsoever to me. We'd been RVing for almost five years and full-timers for seven months. During this rogue Colorado snowstorm in early September, I felt like pulling my 'reluctant' trump card and demanding we high-tail it back home to the warm weather in Florida.

Then I remembered. It'd been only nine weeks since I'd signed the closing documents on my beautiful home and garden back in Tampa. I no longer had a house in Florida. The RV was now the only home I had. I now had no choice but to deal with weather extremes, mechanical failures, and all sorts of other nomadic challenges.

Being stuck inside our RV for three days gave me additional insight into what life must have been like for the hundreds of thousands of Americans during the past six months of the pandemic. Many had been confined inside their homes and apartments, looking out their windows at the same scenes every day. In contrast, I'd spent that time traveling in an RV, changing locations every month or so, and enjoying small mountain towns with great weather and low incidents of the coronavirus.

I could sit here and complain about a little three-day cold snap and the inconvenience of sixty-degree temperatures inside and no running water. I could cringe at how Michael and I must have smelled since neither of us changed our clothes or bathed for three days. I'd been lucky to find a set of long johns at a Walmart, and they were so warm and comfy I wasn't about to take them off, not even for a sponge bath.

I knew I should be asking God to forgive me for carping. I sat in my little RV office, typing away on my laptop and looking out at one of the most beautiful, idyllic snow-covered mountain scenes I could imagine. Through this snowstorm, I'd learned new things about RVing, and I'd added another adventure to our growing list.

I realized I was living a dream, and I was staying healthy and safe. Put into this perspective, becoming a full-time RVer during the pandemic looked like the best decision Michael and I had made in our entire lives.

CHAPTER 17

BIDING TIME

RVing stopped being fun for a while after the Labor Day snowstorm. Although Green Mountain Falls was a charming little town, there was no place to buy groceries or do much of anything other than drink and eat wings at The Blue Moose. As much fun as it might have been to spend hours every day doing just that, we resisted. It was too cold to sit outside on the Blue Moose patio, and the fear of contracting Covid-19 kept us from going inside.

When the weather warmed up again, we searched for good hiking trails. Everyone in nearby Colorado Springs seemed to find the same trails we did. Garden of the Gods was especially popular, but we didn't go back after our first trip. The park had bulged with visitors. We had trouble finding a place to park but no problem finding traffic jams on both the roads and the trails. Too unsafe in terms of social distancing, and half the people weren't wearing masks. Besides, the park was too noisy and open to feel like an outing in a natural area, no matter how real and untouched those huge boulders might have been.

Sandwiched between Woodland Park to the north and Colorado Springs to the south, our RV park sat beside heavily-trafficked U.S. Highway 54. We couldn't get away from the noise and sense of urgency all those cars and trucks communicated as they sped up and down the mountains.

We couldn't leave just yet, however. We'd been waiting five months for service and warranty repairs on our RV at an RV service center in Colorado Springs. We weren't about to skip out on this appointment, no matter how unpleasant the shock of returning to a metropolitan area felt.

Service on the motorhome wasn't the only thing that kept us in the area, though. While Michael and I were in good health for a couple of old geezers in their seventies, we both had issues that occasionally required medical attention. We'd found medical care on the road challenging, more so because our medical concerns fell into chronic as opposed to acute conditions. Since the beginning of this pandemic, we'd wrestled with which might be riskier—ignoring our medical concerns by not going to doctors or sitting in waiting rooms of sick patients, some of whom might infect us with Covid-19.

Before Michael and I took off on this road trip, I'd been under the care of a dermatologist for precancerous skin lesions. A biopsy showed one area as a squamous cell carcinoma. I was in the Rio Grande Valley of South Texas when my Tampa dermatologist's appointment date arrived. I kept looking at the cancerous lesion on the back of my hand and imagined it gnawing deeper and deeper into my flesh. I obsessed about that lesion until I found a dermatologist in McAllen, made an appointment, and let the new doctor perform the surgery.

By the time this road trip landed us in Green Mountain Falls, Colorado, I'd already seen three different dermatologists and had twice begun new rounds of topical chemotherapy. I wasn't ready yet to abandon my latest dermatologist in Frisco, Colorado, regardless of how long the drive might be from Colorado Springs. I insisted we stay in the area until my current inflammations resolved.

Telehealth was one of the few positives that seemed to have come out of the pandemic. For routine issues, Michael and I were able to stay in touch with our regular physicians in Tampa, who were happy to phone in prescription refills to the CVS closest to where we were. However, we did have to risk lab appointments for periodic blood work for doctors to do this. We ignored our newer physical complaints, however, such as my trigger finger and Michael's painful joints. Getting a relief-producing injection into a tendon or having X-rays that'd most likely show arthritis were not worth risking contraction of a deadly virus.

Michael had already chalked up losing a tooth to Covid-19 when we'd been unable to get back to Tampa for a root canal appointment. When the pandemic erupted, we'd been too afraid to go to an unknown dentist in one of the small towns where we'd been staying. When we finally went to a dentist for cleanings and exams, it was too late for the dentist to save Michael's tooth. Michael now refers to the empty spot in his gums as his "Covid gap."

I didn't want my skin to be yet another pandemic casualty. At the same time, I didn't want any of our other medical situations to deteriorate before it felt safe to walk into a physician's office again.

I realized that if a dermatologist I'd seen on the road had diagnosed me with a basal cell carcinoma, I wouldn't have hesitated one moment to walk into a dermatologist's office. Squamous cell cancer, in contrast, was of little consequence when treated within a reasonable amount of time. Another six months or so felt like an acceptable risk. The timeline calmed me.

How much control could an individual have over his mortality? I'd gone for almost an entire year without any medical care, except for one dental examination and cleaning and several dermatology appointments for non-life-threatening skin issues. I had no idea what kinds of other threats lurked in my body. In the overall scheme of life, my skin lesion concerns were diddly-squat.

Singing the blues over poor RV service often happens in the RV community. Throw in a pandemic, and the singing turns into screeching.

Every January, the Tampa Fairgrounds hosts what they brag is 'The World's Largest RV Show.' Michael had been dragging me out to the fairgrounds for this event every year since 2016. "I want to keep up with the industry, see what's new," he'd said. "Plus, it's a great place to find all kinds of RV stuff at low prices."

Our trek to the fairgrounds in 2020 would be different, in any case. We planned to buy a new motorhome. We purchased from a large nationwide chain with over 120 retail outlets for RV sales, parts, and service in thirty-six states. The chain was so large Michael and I dubbed it "The Big C." We naively thought that buying our RV from a large chain would ensure we could receive service all over the country as needed during our travels.

Brand new motorhomes routinely came off assembly lines with problems. We'd planned to identify the issues on our two-month maiden voyage and then have them fixed in Tampa while we emptied and sold our house.

In early April, when we realized we wouldn't go back home anytime soon, Michael started calling Big C stores in Texas, trying to schedule routine maintenance as well as warranty repairs.

"What the hell?" Michael asked. I knew his question was rhetorical. "I've been trying for almost a week, and I can't get a single Big C service manager to return a call." We later read that RV sales during the second and third quarters of 2020 had risen 600%, which explained our difficulties. "We're going to have to select a spot we're willing to travel to and keep trying to get an appointment there. It's not going to be anytime soon, though."

We chose Colorado. After a couple more weeks of repeated calls and left messages, a service manager at the Big C in Colorado Springs finally returned Michael's call. He scheduled our motorhome for service in late September, which would be an almost five-month wait. Later we'd realize how lucky we were to get this far. Some service centers reported delays up to a year for appointments.

We marked our appointment on the calendar and waited our turn.

Our appointment at the Big C finally arrived. Although the Labor Day weekend in Colorado had been cold and snowy, the weather had turned hot again. Temperatures in Colorado Springs now reached the low nineties in the afternoons.

We stayed at a KOA a mile away from our service center. The plan was for us to drop off our RV at 9:00 A.M. and then bring it back to the park at the end of each day. The center would not predict how many days it would take to complete the work.

The RV park scared the bejesus out of us. Few folks wore masks or social distanced, although most of the staff and volunteers did. And if the weather, the challenge of finding things to do for eight hours during the day, and the Covid-19 risks weren't enough to make us unhappy, the KOA sat one block off Interstate 25. The roar of traffic bombarded us nonstop when we were in the park. We hadn't realized how accustomed we'd become to quietness and stillness.

Colorado Springs threw us into culture shock. Except for short stays in New Orleans and San Antonio, we'd spent the past seven months in deserts and small mountainous areas. Until now, we'd felt smug and confident we'd survive this pandemic. But here, fewer than half the shoppers in the grocery stores wore masks, and we routinely saw employees with masks pulled down below their noses and sometimes even under their chins.

The Big C finished its work on a Friday at 5:00 P.M. and almost pushed us out the door. The service manager reported completing all the maintenance and warranty repairs, minus only the replacement of a recliner, which had broken the first time Michael tried to make it recline. We opted not to wait the estimated six weeks for the manufacturer to ship a new one. Other than the recliner, the manager told us everything else was as good as new.

We left Colorado Springs, eager to get out of the searing heat and the urban insanity. We planned to drive directly through New Mexico and then spend a month in Flagstaff, Arizona, on our way to our winter destination in southern California.

During the four days it took us to drive to Flagstaff, we discovered that the technicians at the Big C had failed to address many of the items on the repair list. A basement door latch that didn't engage properly and sometimes popped open on the road appeared untouched and still popped open. Two factory defective mesh pockets in overhead storage bins were neither repaired nor replaced. Not only did the center not fix the dashboard monitor and GPS, but it had also left the unit completely dead, whereas the radio had worked when we'd brought it in for service. They did not install our new $600+ Tire Minder properly, and this system failed to work at all. Most infuriating of all, they did nothing to diagnose our intermittent furnace failure. The service manager said when they'd turned the furnace on, it seemed to work fine, so they moved on. (Two weeks later in Flagstaff, when the temperatures dipped into the upper forties at night, the furnace again didn't work, leaving us in a shivering rage.)

We could only hope the service guys at that Big C center had changed the oil, checked the fluid levels, and inflated the tires to their proper levels. The list of items they actually fixed was short. They'd fixed three broken window shades, replaced a faucet at the kitchen sink, and installed a new showerhead in the bathroom. These minor repairs and replacement parts seem laughable, considering they kept our rig for three long, hot consecutive days. They could have completed those repairs in less than two hours.

Since our Colorado Springs service appointment, Michael has had three different mobile RV mechanics work on our furnace to the tune of almost a thousand dollars. Finally, the last mechanic accurately identified and replaced the malfunctioning part. While we're afraid to exhale too deeply, the furnace has now worked properly for over two months, with regular nightly use.

Prior to the pandemic, we might have considered ourselves urban dwellers at heart. While loving the outdoors, we almost preferred walking down city sidewalks to some of the steep mountain trails that robbed us of oxygen and challenged our endurance.

Running from Covid and biding time in remote areas had changed us. We'd grown to love the quiet spaciousness of sparsely populated places and now felt spooked by the noise, congestion, and chaos of urban areas. After months of looking out our RV windows at gorgeous woods and mountains, I'd said to Michael more than once, "I don't ever want to live again in a place without a view." He agreed.

"I think when the time comes that we have to settle down again, I'd like it to be in a remote area," Michael said.

"But when we have to give up RVing, it'll most likely be because of medical problems, and these small towns won't have doctors, especially not the specialists, that we'll need."

"We'll worry about that when the time comes," my husband said. "Right now, I'm just happy to have the wheels spinning and the open road out the front windshield." And so was I.

I reached another pandemic insight after our RV service experience in Colorado Springs. Just as we were pretty much on our own for medical care, we were also on our own when it came to service for our tin can house. Until the world returned to some semblance of normality, repairs on our RV would be slap-happy and haphazard, at best. I could only hope no trip-stopping mechanical failures or accidents would happen. We vowed to be extra careful.

Meanwhile, we'd keep an eye on that basement door that popped open from time to time, and somewhere down the road, we'd get the dash monitor replaced and our tire pressure monitoring system installed correctly. As nice as these things would have been, they weren't necessary to keep the wheels rolling and new scenery out the front windshield.

Our wheels still turned, and our grins spread from one ear to the other as we sped down Interstate 25, heading out of Colorado.

Our rig under a Mesquite tree in the Rio Grande Valley in south Texas.

My RV office.

Crossing the Rio Grande River to Boquillas del Carmen, Mexico.

Gerri & Michael in Big Bend National Park.

Michael hiking in Cripple Creek, Colorado.

Gerri at a sidewalk cafe in Cripple Creek, Colorado.

Michael & Gerri on the narrow-gauge railroad in Leadville, Colorado.

Gerri hiking at Turquoise Lake in Leadville, Colorado.

Michael hiking at Turquoise Lake in Leadville, Colorado.

Gerri in Aspen grove in Flagstaff, Arizona.

Gerri in Death Valley National Park.

Michael in Death Valley National Park.

Covid didn't catch us!

CHAPTER 18

RUNNING WITH A STICK

Running from the coronavirus began to feel like running with a stick. The image conjured childhood memories of my parents yelling at me not to run with a stick in my hand, that I'd fall and poke my eye out. Now, Michael and I were running, and it felt like any minute we'd trip, fall, and poke our eyes out with airborne Covid-19 particles that would make us very sick and possibly take our lives.

As the pandemic worsened, we ordered food online and drove to grocery store parking lots for curbside pickups. We needed other supplies from time to time, like gasoline for the car and propane for the furnace and the Blue Rhino tank. We deliberated and sweated over every errand. The odds of getting sick felt greater by the day, especially as we heard of more people we knew contracting Covid-19, many of whom struggled long after testing revealed them no longer positive. Several people I knew had died.

At least Michael had stopped talking about his mortality four times a day. I suspected he was keeping his fears to himself rather than talking about them aloud. I hoped we weren't both becoming psychos.

It was the end of September. We'd been on the road, living as fugitives, for over five months. We weren't running from the law, enemies, or some down-and-out family member wanting money. We were running from deadly, invisible viral particles, trying our hardest to avoid this ubiquitous disease. If that wasn't running with a stick, I didn't know what was.

The Colorado Rockies had offered cool nights, pleasant days, and great outdoor options to keep us busy. Although both Cripple Creek and Leadville were tourist areas, we generally found the tourists compliant with masks and social distancing.

The locals in these small mountain towns, however, proved a different ilk. Maybe surviving winters in such a harsh, brutally cold environment had left them stubborn and fiercely independent. After all, if one could survive being snowed in for days in an isolated cabin up in the mountains, perhaps confidence emerged, along with an unwillingness to pay attention to what others were saying or doing. Or to pandemic mandates.

The first time I went into a Dollar Store in Cripple Creek, searching for paper plates, the teenaged clerk stood behind the front register without a mask.

"Aren't you supposed to have a mask on?" I asked.

"Don't have to," he said with a surly snarl. "It's only a mandate, not a law."

His answer stunned me into silence.

A few days later, we waited in line at the Venture Foods grocery store in Cripple Creek. A non-masked clerk came over to ring us up. "Where's your mask?" I asked.

The clerk rolled her eyes. "I'm not even supposed to be out here. You should be glad you're getting service."

Jeez, I thought. I didn't say anything else to her, but her remark rankled. Later in the afternoon, I called the store, asked to speak with the manager, and reported the incident. The manager said he'd investigate and speak with the employee, but I have no idea whether he did. We shopped at the store several more times, and I never saw the woman again. I hoped the manager hadn't fired her. All I wanted was to have employees in stores help me stay healthy as I tried to help them do the same.

"You're being a crotchety old woman," my husband had said.

"Oh, yeah? What if I said I'd done it just for you? You're the one convinced you'll die if you get Covid."

"It's only a matter of time before we're exposed," Michael said. "I've been reading research articles. This country hasn't a clue what it's in for ahead."

"Well, aren't you the optimist?"

"No, really, it's going to get much, much worse before it gets better. You just wait and see."

I feared my very smart husband was right. For months I'd been freaking out when I saw folks in stores without masks. I felt like screaming, "I want to live. Keep your friggin' germs to yourself."

I understood at last that I could not trust others to protect me. Michael and I must assume full responsibility for not contracting Covid-19.

Michael had gone into a mask-buying frenzy. "What are these? More boxes of masks?" I'd just come back from the park office, several boxes in my arms.

"They're going to be in short supply soon. We need to stock up."

"But don't you already have several boxes? Why three more?" I feared my anxious husband was on his way to becoming a hoarder.

"I'm telling you—we'll use every one of them before this is over."

"Doom and gloom," I muttered under my breath. I knew, however, that I, too, had become ridden with anxiety. An underlying sense of dread and finality permeated everything I did. There were times I'd wake up in the middle of the night and bolt to an upright position in bed, my heart pounding and sleep refusing to return. I found myself engaging in dry-run rehearsals of my death, trying out different parting expressions and words, knowing full well my thoughts were pathetic and pathological. I fought a fatalistic feeling that I would not survive this crisis.

I took deep breaths and tried to focus on how lucky I was to be in an RV, isolated except for buying food. I could change the view out my dinette window whenever I wanted. I could go outside in great weather and wike in some of the most pristine and beautiful places on the planet. A balanced diet of fresh food, eight hours of sleep every night, and plenty of fresh air, sunshine, and exercise had left me feeling healthier than I'd felt in years.

I needed to let it go. While I might be metaphorically running with a stick in my hand, I could turn it into a smaller stick by remaining strong and positive. And if I maintained my discipline long enough, maybe I'd live through this nightmare after all.

When we left Colorado, we'd wanted to spend a couple of days in the Albuquerque area. We had friends there and wanted to visit with them over a meal and a few drinks. However, three days before we left Colorado Springs, the Governor of New Mexico issued a mandatory 14-day quarantine for anyone entering the state. "There goes that visit," I'd said to Michael. Instead of stopping for a few days in Albuquerque, we boogie-shoed as fast as we could across New Mexico and into Arizona.

We didn't care where we stayed for the next month, as long as the weather was comfortable. We'd been on the road over eight months, and we again were biding time, trying to stay safe. We headed north to Flagstaff.

We found and nestled into a gorgeous, woodsy campground just outside of town. The place brought home to us the differences between RV parks and campgrounds. We decided to always search for campgrounds in the future. We loved the larger sites, the natural environment, and especially the Ponderosa Pines that surrounded us. We eventually recovered from the hour-long process of getting the damned rig leveled on our tricky, sloped site. We'd even come to shrug at the reverse gravity required to drain our sewer hose uphill rather than down. Such is life, we realized. The beauty of our campsite made it all tolerable.

We loved Flagstaff and had no intention of leaving until the end of the month. The weather was unseasonably warm, and it promised to stay that way through October.

However, the weather did not keep its promise. Just as had happened to us a month earlier in Colorado, meteorologists predicted a sudden cold front and 6-in. of snow. Once again, we found ourselves running from a freezing snowstorm. We couldn't risk damage to the rig from frozen waterlines and pipes, especially now knowing first-hand how difficult RV repairs are during a pandemic.

I hated that we had to leave Flagstaff in a rush. It'd been one of my favorite towns, a place I could easily envision buying a condo and calling it home. We'd felt safe in Flagstaff, but would we in our next destination?

Here we go again, I thought, running with a stick. With every flight, I understood a bit better that Michael and I needed to accept 100% of the responsibility for keeping ourselves safe.

CHAPTER 19

DID LONDON BRIDGE REALLY FALL DOWN?

On the lam, once again from a snowstorm, we scrambled to find a place to hang out during the last week in October. Lake Havasu City, Arizona, looked about halfway between Flagstaff and Desert Hot Springs, our next destination. Of greater importance, the weather there promised warm temperatures and sunny skies. "Why not?" we asked each other. As RVers, we'd been hearing about Lake Havasu for years. Now, we'd see it as well.

Lake Havasu City disappointed us. The town had about 52,000 people and extended for miles along a couple of parallel, heavily-trafficked highways. It sat in the middle of a desert, miles from the next town of any size. The lake, the desert, and the weather were the big draws for the estimated 775,000 visitors who came each year, with boaters and RVers descending in droves during the winter months. No one would choose Lake Havasu City as a summer destination—temperatures soared well over a hundred degrees daily. Except for a short older street of bars, restaurants, and trendy shops, the town held no charm for us. It looked modern and ugly, filled with large chain and big-box stores. RV and boat dealers, repair shops, and storage lots seemed to make up most locally-owned businesses.

The Lake Havasu area also attracted hikers for the many desert trails. Temperatures rose to the nineties during our time there. We never bothered to check out trails, where we might have even been able to hike rather than wike. The terrain was flat, not like the mountainous areas where we'd been the past six months. Even slathered with an SPF-100 sunscreen, I didn't want that blistering sun even on my hands, the only skin I'd have trouble shading or covering.

Our RV resort proved adequate but non-distinct. Sites were small and cramped, with hardly enough space to park the car. Neighbors were aloof. During the week of our stay, we talked only to one guy on one side who traveled alone. He appeared to be a heavy drinker, becoming more friendly in direct proportion to the number of beers he consumed.

The major tourist attraction in Lake Havasu City was the city's London Bridge. "We've got to go see this," I said to Michael. "It must really be huge and impressive."

"How did the London Bridge end up in the middle of the Mohave Desert? That sounds ludicrous."

I shrugged, not yet having an answer.

We hoped we'd find at least one bar or restaurant with outside seating for afternoon happy hours. On our first day in Lake Havasu City, we found a Mexican restaurant with a patio overlooking a narrow water channel. We ordered chips and salsa. Michael had a Heineken, and I splurged on a super-sized Margarita. Our waitress delivered our drinks and pointed out a bridge to us. "That's the London Bridge," she said.

"That's it?" Michael asked. His tone conveyed his shock.

"I guess we drove over it to get here," I said. "I never even noticed a bridge."

"Well, it is kind of small. The Thames River was a lot wider than the Colorado River, and I guess they didn't want to ship that many bricks over here," our waitress said. "But still, you've got to be impressed with the time and effort to ship all this stuff from England out here to the desert."

After the waitress moved on, Michael snorted and said, "That's got to be about the lamest roadside attraction I've ever seen in my life."

"Be nice. They're proud of this bridge."

A friend who used to live in Lake Havasu City told me later my husband would have liked the bridge a lot better if we'd been there during the summer. "Women go down to the little beach beside the bridge and sunbathe topless," my friend said.

The London Bridge was the only thing I'd seen so far in Lake Havasu I'd found even mildly interesting. As we were leaving, I said, "I'm going to do some research on this bridge when we get back to the rig." I wondered when, if ever, I'd start referring to the rig as home.

The history of both Lake Havasu and the London Bridge piqued my interest. Without the lake, there would never have been a bridge. Engineers had created Lake Havasu from the Colorado River, and the lake had inspired the founder of Lake Havasu City to buy the bridge.

The Colorado River is a 1,450-mile watershed originating in northern Colorado and draining into the Pacific Ocean after running south through seven U.S. states and two Mexican states. To provide water to the surrounding desert, the government appropriated funds during the early 1930s to construct the Parker Dam along the Colorado River. The dam construction created Lake Havasu, which holds 211 billion gallons of water and borders over 450 miles of shoreline. On the western side, the lake serves as the border between Arizona and California.

During the seventeenth century, England built a series of wooden bridges over the Thames River. At the time of their construction, the bridges needed only to be strong enough to hold the weight of foot traffic, horses and carriages, and horse-drawn wagons of goods. Over time, these wooden bridges deteriorated, and workers replaced them with solid stone bridges.

English workers completed the construction of the solid brick London Bridge in 1831. Due to population increases and heavier traffic, the bridge began deteriorating and sinking into the ground. The invention of automobiles in the late 1800s sealed the demise of this solid stone structure, as it did with the entire series of British bridges that crossed the Thames. By the time this bridge was officially retired, the bridge's east side was 3-4" lower than the west side due to deterioration.

In 1967, London started looking for a buyer for the bridge. The founder of Lake Havasu City, Robert P. McCulloch, Sr., learned of the opportunity. He viewed the novel purchase of the London Bridge as a unique marketing strategy to encourage folks to move to his newly-created town in the desert. In 1968, McCulloch paid $2.4 million for the bridge. Workers in England dismantled it, numbering and labeling all the bricks as they removed them. Ships brought the bricks from England through the Panama Canal and unloaded them in Long Beach, California. Trucks then hauled them to Arizona.

While appearing to be a perfect replica, the re-created London Bridge did not follow the original British design on the interior. Engineers had found that hollow, steel-reinforced bridges held heavier loads and lasted longer than their solid-brick predecessors. In keeping with contemporary specifications, the Lake Havasu London Bridge contains steel beams inside its brick facade.

"Listen to this, Michael." I'd just read something about the bridge that tickled my brain. "They re-constructed this bridge on solid land. Then they dredged out a channel and routed water from Lake Havasu to go under the bridge. How weird is that?"

Michael, deeply immersed in his two-hour daily dose of current events, didn't respond.

"Well, I guess it gives an extended meaning to the 'build it, and they will come' theory. Build a bridge, and the water will come." I chuckled at my creativity, which may or may not have been particularly creative.

To complete his charming little English touch to Lake Havasu City, McCulloch created a small replica of an English village at one end of the bridge. The open-air mall included a few outside restaurants and bars, a candle shop, a couple of gift shops, and a replica of an old fire-engine red English telephone booth.

Town officials formally dedicated the London Bridge in 1971, three years after McCulloch bought it. The town celebrated the 50th anniversary of the bridge's purchase in October 2018. The festivities ended with a traditional 'sheep-crossing' across the bridge. The waterway underneath the bridge is the Bridgewater Channel. What a cute little name, I thought.

According to our waitress at the Mexican restaurant, people came from all over the world to see Lake Havasu's London Bridge and to have their pictures taken on it, under it, and beside it. While it was a very cool thing to experience, the London Bridge would not become our strongest memory of Lake Havasu City. Not by a long shot.

We stayed in Lake Havasu City from October 24 until November 1, 2020. The 2020 Presidential Election was heating up, big time. We'd arrived in this southwestern edge of Arizona after weeks in northern Arizona, a historically Republican state promising a very close race between Donald Trump and Joe Biden. In Flagstaff, a university town and a liberal area, we felt little of the upcoming election pressures or controversies. Politics simply were not even apparent.

We found a very different political climate in Lake Havasu than what we'd experienced in Flagstaff. Here, Trump banners, bumper stickers, Maga baseball caps, and t-shirts were everywhere. Campaign activities and materials bombarded us everywhere we went. We never once saw a Biden bumper sticker, t-shirt, or promotional material of any sort.

Strolling through the English Village at the foot of the London Bridge on a Sunday morning walk, we noticed a gift shop displaying dozens of large Trump/Pence banners. Nada a one for Biden and Harris. A short distance later, we met a couple about our ages walking towards us, the man wearing a Trump t-shirt.

I cringed as my husband stopped the couple and asked, "I'm curious. How come all those Trump banners they're selling back there are blue?"

The man looked startled. And didn't answer. The woman, however, laughed and said, "That's the best one I've heard yet."

My husband grinned as we continued our walk.

After the election, I looked up the election results for Arizona and the breakdown by county. Mohave County, where Lake Havasu City is located, voted for Trump over Biden 75.0% to 23.7%. This result was the highest percentage of votes for the Republican candidate in the entire state. Overall, Biden led the final Arizona vote 49.4% compared to Trump's 49.1%. Lake Havasu City had been the largest, strongest Trump stronghold in Arizona. It helped me understand the political inundation we'd felt while there.

We arrived at our Xscapers California Home Base in Desert Hot Springs, California, on November 1st, long before officials certified the Presidential election results. During that first week in California, as Michael and I stayed glued to CNN, ABC, and other news sources to find out which candidate would win the official electoral college vote, a fellow RVer in our sheltered group in the back-forty of this lovely desert RV park warned us, "Do not talk politics in this group. It's an unspoken rule. Politics are not important inside this bubble, and it's not cool to bring the subject up. Keep your political preferences to yourself."

While this advice possibly sent my husband into paroxysms of despair, I sighed in relief. Somehow this election had exhausted me, and all I'd had to do personally was send my mail-in ballot to the Supervisor of Elections back in Florida. My husband, in contrast, inhaled CNN as if it were the oxygen his life required.

I've thought a lot about our time in Lake Havasu City that week that preceded the 2020 Presidential Election. I wasn't sure I'd ever been in such a politically-charged and committed atmosphere. Although I'd felt freaked-out while we were there, like maybe this territory was a bit too foreign for me, in retrospect, I think it helped me better understand the zeitgeist of our country. People care, and they care deeply. Maybe that's the most critical take-away anyone could have.

CHAPTER 20

WHAT'S FOR DINNER?

Cooking a decent dinner in an RV has been a chronic RV challenge for us. While not exactly foodies, we like fresh, healthy, and well-prepared meals. Eating is one of our greatest pleasures. We enjoy everything about it, or at least we used to. The coronavirus outbreak changed that.

On the road, before Covid-19, we'd eat out a couple of times a week. At home, we'd usually go out about once a week. We didn't do fine dining, but neither did we eat drive-through fast food. We gravitated toward Italian food, and a chain like Macaroni Grill or Olive Garden satisfied our palettes and levels of sophistication just fine. Occasionally I could talk Michael into either seafood or Mexican food. He liked Asian, and periodically he'd convince me to go to a chain like Pei Wei for a change of pace. Although we knew it wasn't healthy, sometimes we even settled for bar food.

We didn't realize when we ate at the la Kiva Restaurant & Bar in Terlingua, Texas, in early March that it'd be the last time we'd eat in a restaurant for a very long time.

"Wish I could remember what I had to eat," I said. "If I'd known it would be like The Last Supper, I'd have written down what we ordered."

"It wasn't about the food anyway," Michael said. "It was about the atmosphere—all the stone walls and floors, the bar, the acoustic musician sitting on that stool and playing. I can still see our table."

"And I remember the dim lighting and that long oak bar that lined the back wall. That bartender surely made a strong Margarita."

Eight months later, when we watched a Netflix documentary called "Texas: The Badlands," we were amazed to see the la Kiva Bar featured in the film. "We were there," I'd said, and we high-fived each other.

When we first heard about Covid-19 and saw footage of Chinese people in masks, we agreed we needed to stay out of crowded restaurants and bars. Occasionally we'd risk outdoor seating in mid-afternoon for a couple of beers and wings. We wanted to live, but risking infection and possible death for a restaurant-cooked meal didn't seem worth it.

When the third upsurge of cases exploded in November, we declared our outside, middle-of-the-afternoon happy hours off-limits. We needn't have bothered with our little declarations, however. We were in the Palm Springs, California area, and all the restaurants closed their patios and shifted to carry-out only, per orders from the California Governor.

"You know, I wouldn't even mind eating at home all the time if we could figure out how to make a decent meal in this thing. I'd be happy with even a slight approximation to what we used to make in our large kitchen back home."

"You've got to stop saying things like that," my husband said. "This is home."

"It's just that I don't think we improved our kitchen area one bit with this new, bigger RV. The only thing different between this one and the last one is a bit more counter space and a couple more cabinets to store stuff in."

"The sink is a lot bigger, and don't forget we have room now to leave the coffee maker and the toaster oven on the counter. Remember in the smaller rig how we had to move them to the bed every time we tried to cook dinner?"

"Well, the stove and oven are just like the ones we had before. The oven continues to be totally useless for anything other than storing pots and pans. How inane to think anyone would get down on the floor and contort themselves to light that darned pilot light at the back of the oven every time they wanted to bake something."

We thought we'd resolved these challenges when we bought a nice toaster oven and an even nicer electric frypan. But no, my cornbread continued to overcook on the edges and remain doughy in the center when baked in the toaster oven. My dumplings in my favorite Chicken and Dumplings recipe continued to come out hard and flat when simmered in the electric frypan.

"What is wrong with me, Michael? How have I forgotten how to cook?"

My husband only shrugged.

In mid-November, now settled for the winter in Desert Hot Springs, I decided to try again with Chicken and Dumplings, one of my quintessential comfort foods.

"These are perfect," Michael said, digging in for seconds on the dumplings. "You're back."

The next morning, I had a revelation. "Do you think the elevation might have had something to do with those dumplings coming out the way they were supposed to? We've been in the mountains all summer at elevations of nine and ten thousand feet. Now we're in the desert at an elevation of 1,076-ft." I'd just looked up our elevation on my phone.

"Could be," Michael said. "Maybe we should have Chili and cornbread for dinner again soon."

We did, and the cornbread rose and cooked in the middle just like it was supposed to.

How was I supposed to know about cooking at high elevations? I'd lived most of my adult life in Tampa, Florida, elevation 48-ft. above sea level. I refused to let myself feel stupid over this one.

I also needed to let go of putting all the blame on the RV kitchen.

Another ongoing frustration of RV travel is trying to find familiar items in new grocery stores. Throw in a pandemic, and the stress rose.

First, there were shortages due to hoarding, especially on paper goods like toilet paper and paper towels. Next came the small but scary interruption of our food supply when Covid-19 cases erupted in several meat production plants. Suddenly we couldn't get pork chops, ham steaks, or bacon.

Next, the delivery of produce seemed to jam up, and we found ourselves unable to find a head of lettuce that looked fresh. We found bare shelves in the supermarkets where pasta and rice were supposed to be. Next came the hoarding and subsequent inability to find bleach, hand sanitizer, and cleaning products like Lysol or Pine-Sol. (We couldn't put those items into our RV tanks, but we could certainly have used them to disinfect surfaces.)

"Well, crap," Michael said. He'd just returned from the store to pick up a can of diced tomatoes so I could make Chili for dinner. "Went to three different stores, and they were all out of diced tomatoes."

We often found ourselves having to scrounge through the pantry, trying to figure out what kind of dinner we could throw together minus an essential item or two we needed for a specific recipe.

But we made do, and we didn't complain, at least not too much. We were still eating balanced diets of homecooked meals with few additives. We were not subjecting ourselves to the risk of going out to eat.

As the pandemic raged and scientists released more data, we began to realize that even going inside a grocery store posed risks, even though we consistently wore KN95 masks when we shopped.

"Think we ought to start ordering online?" Michael asked.

I didn't have an answer. "I don't know. I really like to pick out my own stuff, particularly the fruits and vegetables."

"I do, too," Michael said, "but I'm thinking we should give it a try. There's no extra charge, and they bring it right to your car in the parking lot when it's ready for pickup."

"Okay. We've got a pretty long list already. Want to give it a try?"

We were in Lake Havasu City at the time, and our RV park was only a couple of miles from a Safeway Supermarket.

We talked a bit more about menus, adding ingredients for a couple more meals to the list, and Michael got to work. Safeway's online shopping site showed pictures of the store's entire inventory, meaning that we could select a bottle of shampoo from the thirty-seven brands the store carried. However, Michael quickly realized that scrolling through seven different brands of kidney beans and then choosing either regular, low sodium or no sodium, selecting either dark or light beans, and then having to decide whether to go for regular or organic, took perhaps more patience than he had cultivated in his seventy years.

Two and a half hours later, my husband announced, "Finally, I'm done. The order will be ready for pickup between three and seven this afternoon. They'll text me when it's ready."

"Jeez, if it's seven, then we're not having Chili for dinner tonight. It takes at least a couple of hours to do all the chopping and for it to cook."

"Well, I did the best I could do. Next time you can do the ordering."

"Do I have to? I thought you did a fine job." I certainly wasn't trying to be critical, but I understood his snappy retort. Patience wasn't one of my strengths either.

The text for pickup of our order came at 6:15 P.M., and we drove together to the Safeway. We called the number posted on the sign, and ten minutes later, an employee named Kristen pushed out a big cart with our groceries. An older guy, also uniformed, walked with her to our car. "He had to come with me since you had beer in the order. I'm not old enough to sell alcohol," Kristen said. The two of them, mostly Kristen, packed the many bags into the car. Michael tried to tip her, but she refused, saying the store didn't allow her to accept tips.

Michael examined the three computer-generated pages of our order after getting back to the rig and unpacked everything. "Look at this, will you? There are no chicken thighs. Says they were 'out of stock.' How the hell does a supermarket run out of chicken thighs?"

I'd also noticed that while I had put two McIntosh apples on the list, the order came with two bags of McIntosh apples.

We tried online ordering a few more times in different towns and with varying supermarket chains. One time we ended up with plastic salad plates when we'd clearly ordered Dixie dinner-sized paper plates. Invariably there'd be a few missing items with every order pickup. Another time Michael ordered one 3-oz. bottle of soy sauce, and we ended up with two 6-oz. bottles of soy sauce. (We threw one of them into a holiday food drive basket. We weren't going to live long enough to use up 6-oz. of soy sauce.)

After a few more orders and curbside deliveries, I began to realize that teenagers were doing the in-store shopping. I had to ask, "What do teenagers know about picking out tomatoes or a head of lettuce?" My mother had taught me those things as a kid, but that was decades ago, back on the farm. During that era, the 4-H Club had been the mainstay of my childhood social life, and The Future Homemakers of America the proffered role for my future.

We abandoned online ordering with reluctance. We knew going into stores increased our likelihood of catching the virus, but the teenaged shoppers made too many mistakes.

As Thanksgiving approached, the pandemic escalated even further. We reconsidered. "Maybe we should order all our staples, canned goods, and stuff like that online. Then we could run in real quick and pick out the meats and produce in person," Michael said. "What do you think of that idea?"

I sighed and said, "I don't know."

But, in truth, I did know. I wanted to enjoy food again. I wanted to go to restaurants and sit inside when the weather was too hot, cold, or windy. I wanted to plan meals and find every friggin' thing I needed during one shopping trip to one store. I never wanted another teenybopper picking out a cucumber or an orange again for me for the rest of my life. I wanted this pandemic to end and my life to go back to normal.

Then I realized it'd never return to normal. We'd sold the house. We'd pulled up and discarded most of our Tampa roots. I no longer had a normal.

I looked around at our socially distanced, masked RV park in Desert Hot Springs, California, and realized this was my normal.

"What's for dinner tonight?" Michael asked.

"Hmm," I said. "Let me look in the fridge and the cabinets and see what I can cobble together."

Michael shrugged but didn't complain. It was the best we could do, and we both knew it.

CHAPTER 21

PAPER DOLLS AND PANDEMICS

I thought after over four years, forty-nine states, five Canadian Provinces, and 50,000 miles of RVing, I knew about RV travel. After all, we'd spent four to six months on the road every year, beginning in late 2015. When we took off on our planned two-month road trip in early 2020, I didn't expect any surprises, other than quirks in the new rig that we'd later have a service center repair under warranty.

When we arrived at our 2020 Xscaper California Home Base, I wasn't sure what we'd find. We'd been on the road nine months, the past six of them in relative isolation. Michael and I had become comfortable in our social and physical detachment with only occasional contact with others in grocery stores or RV offices.

As we pulled into our new site in the RV park club section, I felt excited and nervous. We wouldn't know for a while whether we'd made a good choice coming to southern California, even if we were in a remote area in the middle of the desert. The Escapees, the large RV club we'd joined in February at the RVillage Rally in north Florida, described this subgroup of the Xscapers as a younger group, most of whom both worked and RVed full-time.

"Younger people aren't as scared as us older folks are," I'd said to Michael. "Even if they got the virus, they probably wouldn't die."

"I'm more concerned about the partying that might go on," Michael said. "Remember those photos from their last Convergence, with all the dancing and partying that reportedly went on all night long?"

"Yeah, but if they're mostly in their 40s and 50s, aren't there likely to be children in the group? I don't think most parents carry on like that when they have kids."

"Well, I'd guess that most of those folks are celebrating their empty nest status, that they've waited for their kids to leave home before going full-time. Even a forty-year-old could easily have adult children," Michael said.

"I can't imagine how difficult it'd be for a child living full-time in an RV during this pandemic. Guess they spend several hours a day online with school, though. Still . . ."

"Guess we'll find out about all these questions before long," Michael said.

Our Home Base hosts met us at the park gate and led us to our site. They all wore masks. Our initial impression was one of conscientiousness about social distancing and safety. We were among the first of the group to arrive and had an end fencerow all to ourselves for a few more days. I felt myself relax, especially as the day began to end and I saw the most beautiful sunset over the mountains I'd ever seen in my life. Whether I liked or fit in with these Xscapers or not, we'd picked a gorgeous place to hunker down during the pandemic.

After all these months on the road, untethered and with only a minimal amount of interaction with other people, I found myself thinking of my early years of isolation on a farm in North Florida, twenty miles from the Georgia State line.

When I was two, my family had loaded everything it owned on the back of an old three-quarter-ton flatbed truck and settled on a 160-acre tract of farmland in Madison County, Florida. Although I was too young to remember the move, I imagine we must have looked like the Joad family from John Steinbeck's *Grapes of Wrath*.

Our four-room clapboard house was two miles from the closest neighbors. Until I entered the public school system at age six, the only time I saw other children was at church on Sundays and Wednesdays. My older brother had no interest in playing with a little sister. Both parents stayed busy with farm chores and had little time or energy to pay much attention to me.

With so many quiet hours alone, I learned to entertain myself. My mom gave me scissors and old Sears Roebuck catalogs. I'd cut out paper dolls and create elaborate houses and towns from the paper figures. I remember my amazement when I received my first book of real paper dolls, the kind with clothes to dress the dolls, using white tabs to make the clothes stay on.

Did anyone play with such low-tech, humble toys anymore? Not having any little girls or their mothers in my current world to ask, I went to Amazon and googled 'paper dolls.'

I learned that today folks consider paper dolls trendy. The 'vintage' paper dolls made of paper are often of fairy tale or Disney characters. Amazon offered paper dolls of princesses, like Cinderella, Elsa, and Rapunzel, as well as paper dolls of horses and puppies. They all came with clothes and accessories, including the animals. However, most of Amazon's paper dolls were not made of paper. They were magnetic, and neither the dolls, the clothes, nor the accessories needed scissors. Little girls now just peeled them off laminated pages.

I found RVing during a pandemic almost as lonely and isolated as that farm in North Florida had been, despite staying in RV parks and campgrounds with other rigs just yards away. Because folks were living nearby didn't mean we talked with them. With Covid-19 cases on the rise, we viewed every fellow camper as a possible Typhoid Mary, and our fellow RVers probably viewed us in the same way.

Michael and I fell into routines. He settled into hours of CNN, You-Tube videos, movies, and concerts, all with his headphones covering his ears. I settled into hours at my laptop, either researching information for my book or merely writing narrative and dialogue off the top of my head. Either way, I worked in silence, my mind wandering, exploring, and occasionally creating. The world outside had little impact on my internal psyche, other than angst over having had my entire former world turned upside down by a coronavirus that should have triggered consistent national intervention but didn't.

We found the Xscapers Home Base unlike anything we'd ever experienced on the road before. We were among the newbies as far as RVing was concerned. Our hosts, cohosts, and many other participants had lived in their rigs full time for years. Most of these rigs had elaborate electronic systems to ensure their devices always had internet connections. They also sported $10,000 solar systems to ensure their rigs always had power.

One of our greatest surprises was to learn that most of these nomadic Xscapers could hardly wait to leave this RV resort. They longed to return to a Bureau of Land Management (BLM) site to set up their rigs in the middle of nowhere. The BLM allowed two to three weeks of continuous boondocking in one place, and most of our neighbors craved that kind of solitude. Sometimes these independent souls traveled in 'pods' of several rigs and boondocked near each other, but they always respected distance and privacy. They neither needed nor wanted social interactions and physical proximity to others, but they seemed to appreciate the safety and security of having kindred souls nearby. They seemed happy and contented in their self-containment.

I began to realize my childhood experiences on a farm in social isolation had perhaps prepared me for a socially isolated existence during the pandemic. The longer we maintained our social distance, the easier I found it. At times, Michael seemed to get bored and restless, and he'd take off around the campground to find someone he could talk with outside for a few minutes. I didn't. The longer I stay alone, the more difficult it became to make myself go out and talk with others.

Should I have worried that I'd lose any social skills I might have had? That I'd become a recluse? That, like these new Xscaper neighbors, I might grow to eschew RV parks and campgrounds?

I wasn't that worried. A vaccine was around the corner, and the country would recover. Rosy predictions for 2021 filled the news. The economy would boom, the virus would disappear, and jobs and prosperity would return. I shrugged, confident that our current circumstances wouldn't last much longer.

Still, I couldn't shake thoughts of those paper dolls I'd seen on Amazon. I realized that sitting at my laptop today wasn't that different from playing with paper dolls on the back stoop as a five-year-old child.

I can do this pandemic, I thought. I've done this before. I resolved to remember my paper doll childhood the next time I felt my ability to wear a mask and social distance from others waver.

CHAPTER 22

THIS MASK IS MAKING ME STUPID

"I hate this thing!" Tears welled in my eyes, and I clenched my fists in frustration. "I can't see. I can't hear. I can't even think with this thing on."

"What are you talking about?" Michael asked. "Sure, they're a little uncomfortable, but it's a small price to pay for staying alive." I found myself suddenly hating my husband for his goddamn calm, adult response.

"You don't understand. The thing is disorienting, downright discombobulating." I was loading groceries into the back of the car, my mask now off my face and stuffed in a pocket in my fanny pack. "I couldn't find the Ajax, the McIntosh apples, a friggin' bar of unscented Dove soap. When is this ever going to end?"

"You know the answer to that—it'll end when this country gets a handle on the coronavirus pandemic," my sane, rational husband said.

Surely, I wasn't the only one going crazy and dumb during this crisis. I wondered what else would happen today to make me feel bad about myself.

*

"Let's go find that nature preserve everyone's talking about," Michael said. "That'll cheer you up." We'd gotten home, unpacked the groceries, minus the items I was too stupid to find, and were now talking about

out how to spend the rest of the afternoon. I was learning that living full-time in an RV, with little to do other than read, write, work Sudoku, and watch Netflix, could sometimes feel challenging, and this happened to be one of those times. I relied on my driven, Type A personality to keep me somewhat productive at my laptop every morning. Except for those hours of writing, I just drifted along, whichever way the wind blew me. Today that wind was blowing me near the end of my rope with this pandemic. I wanted my life back.

"Okay. Want to drive or want me to?"

"You drive," Michael said. "Everything's set up for you." We'd discovered a real problem with being a one-car family living in an RV. Every time we switched drivers, the driver had to readjust the driver's seat and the mirrors. Maybe my husband sensed that my agitation level was a bit above normal today and that it might further irritate me if I had to wait for him to readjust everything.

I pulled out of the RV park and turned right on Dillon Road. "How far is it supposed to be?" I asked.

"Folks are saying just drive east about fifteen minutes until we see a huge grove of palm trees. That'll be where the San Andreas Fault line is, and that's where the hiking trails are."

Traffic was sparse, and most of it looked like locals in pickup trucks or service vehicles. The automobiles moved at a clip, though, and occasionally it felt like they were going a hundred as they approached or passed me.

The speed limit was 55 mph, and the road looked and felt like a mini roller coaster as we went up and down. Although not steep enough to trigger a rush, the sense of falling off a cliff nevertheless overtook me at each crest. The grades were high enough to prevent seeing what lay on the other side. Large brownish-gray mountains rose in the distance, an occasional one with a white snowcap. On both sides of the road, rocky sand undulated in the intense desert sun. We were in the Coachella Valley at the northern end of the Colorado Desert, two hours east of Los Angeles.

I drove for what felt like an hour. "Do you think we've missed it? Why don't you google it on your phone?"

Michael pulled out his cellphone and started pecking. I was ready to turn the car around and head back home.

Michael jerked upright in his seat. "Think that highway patrolman is going to turn around and chase you down?"

"What are you talking about? I didn't see a patrolman. Besides, I wasn't speeding."

"Are you kidding me? You were going seventy in a 55-mph zone."

"Well, maybe I got a little above the limit, but they can't use radar from the other direction," I said. I did, however, turn the car around and set the cruise control to fifty-five, just in case.

Within minutes, I saw the patrolman behind me, red lights flashing.

"Shit," I said. "He did turn around." I eased over to the shoulder, rolled down the window, and asked Michael to get the registration and insurance information out of the glove compartment.

As the officer approached, I fumbled in my pockets, trying to find a mask, then realized it was in my fanny pack. I mumbled to the officer that I was looking for my mask, and he waved his hand, saying it wasn't necessary. He wasn't wearing one, and he stood less than six feet from my open window. I kept looking for my mask, found it, and put it on. Later I'd wonder if this mere act of putting on a mask might have offended the officer and triggered what ensued. Or again, maybe that damned mask just made me too stupid to realize that I started this interchange with noncompliance with a law enforcement officer's directive.

I only know as I sat there trembling in the driver's seat on the shoulder of the road, I was scared. I hadn't gotten a speeding ticket in thirty-five years. I had Safe Driver on my license. I'd updated all the necessary documentation of driver's license, registration, and insurance to the appropriate legal residency address in Florida several months earlier when we became full-time RVers. Everything was in order. How could I have been so oblivious to my surroundings and gone 15 mph over the limit?

I handed the patrolman the registration and insurance card. "Driver's license?" he asked.

"Yes, sir." I could have slapped my forehead. Of course. The license was the most important thing, and I'd forgotten about it. I wasn't thinking straight. I fumbled in my fanny pack and handed my license to him.

"Do you know how fast you were going?"

"I know it was over fifty-five. I'm so sorry."

"What's the rush? Where are you headed in such a hurry?"

I started trying to explain how we were looking for the nature preserve, had realized we'd gone too far, and had been looking for a place to turn around. Michael jumped into the conversation, backing up my story but adding all kinds of additional information I viewed as completely irrelevant and unnecessary. Details such as us being full-time RVers, where we were staying, the name of the group we were with, how long we planned to be in the area. I felt like telling him to shut up. I was the driver. This interview should have been between the highway patrolman and me, not with my loquacious husband interrupting and talking over me.

After what felt like five long minutes, the patrolman turned back to me. Then came the barrage: "Where are you from? How long have you been driving? Don't you think you should've been paying attention to your speed? Why weren't you thinking about the safety of others, of your husband, of yourself? Do you think you deserve a ticket?"

At this last question, my jaw dropped down. What the hell was I supposed to say to that? "Well, probably I do, sir. I broke the law."

He leaned down and asked Michael, "Do you think I should give her a ticket? It'd be for $300. That's the California cost when you're going fifteen or more mph over the speed limit."

I held my breath, wondering if my husband would come to my defense. He said, "She was speeding. It's not up to me, but I'll make sure she pays it if you give her one."

You jerk, I thought. I felt like screaming. "You'll make sure of nothing pertaining to me and my life. You're not my boss!" He could have at least backed me up, said something like 'she usually stays at the limit,' or 'I'm not sure why she wasn't using the cruise control today,' or 'she's never gotten a speeding ticket during the entire time I've known her.' I fumed.

Returning to face me, the officer's onslaught of circular, rhetorical questions continued. "How can I know you won't do this again? Why do you think California has speed limits? Do you have any idea how dangerous this road is with all its blind hills? What if you had hurt someone?"

My agitation increased with every blustered, stammered answer I gave. Finally, "Sir, I was wrong to drive so fast. I understand, and I accept whatever decision you make. Please believe me when I say I respect rules and laws. They hold society together." My volume and rate of speech increased. Hoping I'd not lose control, I continued. "I spent forty years as a public service employee. Trust me—I know how to follow the rules, and I believe everyone should."

"What kind of work did you do?"

"I was a social worker, and thirty of the years were in a public school system. I was regularly subjected to criminal background checks, arrest records, and drug screenings. This is as much trouble as I've ever been in in my life."

"No kidding," he said. "My wife's a social worker. She works with hospice."

I didn't say anything.

"Okay," he said. "I want you to give me five reasons why you think you've learned your lesson about not speeding."

I hesitated, trying to come up with five reasons this idiot might believe so he'd let me go. By this point, I wanted to say, "Just write the damn ticket." It would almost be worth $300 to get out of this baking sun and drive away. He'd humiliated me long enough.

Instead, I said, "Number 1: I broke the law, and now I feel bad about myself. Number 2: I put lives in danger with my reckless behavior. Number 3: I feel guilty, and I don't like the feeling. Number 4: This talk is going to stay with me much longer than paying the ticket would, and Number 5 . . ." and my mind went blank.

He waited, and we lapsed into a stare-down of sorts. Finally, "I can't think of anything else." I'm not sure how long we looked into each other's eyes. I only knew I'd reached my limit. I could talk to this man no longer.

"Wait here." He turned and walked back to his patrol car. Through the rearview mirror, I saw him pull a pad out of his pocket, place it on the car roof, and pull out his ballpoint pen.

"He's writing something," I said to Michael.

"You're f_cked," he said. "They don't write anything down unless it's a ticket."

I wasn't sure what to think, but I did register that he hadn't gotten into his car to run a computer check on my information. He hadn't checked out my driver's license to see if it was valid. He hadn't pulled up my driving history, verified the insurance and registration information, nor determined whether there was an outstanding warrant for my arrest somewhere. He'd done none of the things I assumed law enforcement routinely did when they stopped a motorist. These had to be good signs, but at that moment, I didn't care. I was too angry.

The highway patrolman came back to my car and handed me a warning ticket. "I want you to promise to keep this on your dash, pin it up on a wall in your house, or put it somewhere where you'll see it every day."

I didn't say anything.

"Well?" he asked. "Should I tear it up and write you a $300 ticket instead?"

"No, sir. I'll leave it right here on the console." I could only hope he didn't realize my small hybrid car had a gear shift where most cars have a console.

"Okay," he said and smiled. "Here are your license and registration." His radio on his belt blared, and I could tell the call distracted him as he tried to listen and talk to me at the same time. "Sounds like some idiot is making trouble over on Interstate 25. I need to go chase this down now. Don't speed again," he said as he headed back to his car.

I quickly rolled up the car window, hoping the temperature would cool down inside soon. That patrolman had rattled me so badly it took a few minutes to locate the additional registration information that had fallen to the floor and clip it to the documents the officer had just returned.

"Jerk," I muttered. I eased out on the highway, built up speed, and set the cruise control at a righteous 55 mph.

"You didn't handle that very well," my husband said.

"What the hell are you talking about?"

"He wanted you to beg and plead and then say thank you."

"What would it take for you to just one time, just once, take my side in a situation?" I feared my blood was about to boil over or my body would spontaneously combust.

"What do you mean? I have no idea what you're talking about. I'm just pointing out that you missed all his cues and didn't say what he wanted you to say."

I took a couple of deep breaths and didn't say a word. Fifteen minutes of silence later, as we finally pulled up to the nature preserve for our afternoon hike, I asked my husband, "Did I get a speeding ticket this afternoon?"

"Well, no."

"Right, so you can keep whatever other thoughts you might have about this afternoon to yourself. I don't want to hear them."

I probably ground another layer of enamel off my teeth that afternoon, furious at both that state trooper and my husband. What kind of friggin' power trip was that officer on? I'd done nothing to deserve having him speak to me as if I were a child. I saw nothing to justify his degradation and humiliation of me. I'd been respectful, deferential, repentant. While I hadn't groveled, neither had I become defensive or argumentative. In my opinion, he was out of line to have spent twenty minutes scolding, chastising, and flaunting his authority over me. I was almost old enough to be his grandmother, and he had not shown me one iota of respect.

And my dear husband, the sanctimonious one who was always right? The one who was forever correcting, instructing, and criticizing? I didn't even try to find the words to describe how I felt.

I pouted the rest of the afternoon and into the night. It'd been a dreadfully infuriating afternoon, and I wasn't going to let it go until I was good and ready. At least I now had an answer to the question I'd asked that morning about what else could make me feel bad about myself.

The following day, I had an insight into my reaction. My mask must have made me crazy. I had failed to think of reason #5, failed to grasp that the officer had wanted me to beg, and I couldn't even see how much smarter my hubby was than me.

God only knows how dumb I'd become if this coronavirus pandemic didn't end soon.

CHAPTER 23

BLOWING IN THE WIND

Bob Dylan's classic protest song from the 1960s, "Blowing in the Wind," has always been one of my favorites. Several things made me think of this song during our 2020 Xscapers California Winter Home Base stay in Desert Hot Springs, California.

"Jeez, this wind is harsh." We woke up during our second week with the Xscapers and heard the wind howling. The rig rocked and swayed. When I peered out the window, it looked as if the palm trees would snap in half. My RV office gave me an elevated view of the campground, complete with the towering San Jacinto Mountains to the southwest. The winds felt and sounded almost hurricane force. Coming from Florida, I understood sixty and seventy mph winds.

Folks had warned us of strong Santa Ana winds in the Coachella Valley, and this was our first experience with them. I assumed the winds were coming from the Pacific Ocean about a hundred miles to the west. The local weather forecast had said a cold front was on its way.

Indications of nest-building had started appearing in the section of the campground where management had assigned the Xscapers. We'd see a potted plant here, wind chimes over there, and an occasional tent or canopy for outside sun protection. With the deliberate spacing of rigs leaving an empty site between each site, we all began spreading out, at times encroaching on the space between our rigs.

Our neighbors to the front had erected a 10-ft. octagonal tent beside their Class A and set up an outside office inside it. We'd heard the guy was an avid Dungeons and Dragons player, which he reportedly played for hours while his younger wife worked full-time online inside their rig. When we'd walk by, we'd see him hunched over a table in his tent, staring at his computer screen, headphones covering his ears.

Suddenly, following a powerful gust, I saw movement out of the corner of my eye. A large nylon structure was tumbling across the flat desert campground floor. "Wow," I said. "Michael, come look at this."

A couple of neighbors, closer than we were, raced out of their rigs to grab the runaway, flyaway octagonal tent. With assistance, our neighbor repositioned the tent over his table, chair, and computer and then found large rocks to weigh down the tent around the bottom edges.

A short time later, we heard a noise on our patio. We looked out to see our four lawn chairs toppled over and six feet from where we'd left them. I felt unnerved, a little scared.

"I sure hope these winds don't damage our rig," I said. "That'd be a pain. Does our insurance cover wind damage?"

"Don't be hysterical," my husband said.

On our afternoon walk later in the day, we noticed that every camper who'd set up a tent had taken it down. "Glad we didn't order a tent from Amazon," Michael said. "Looks like it'd be a real pain in the ass if these winds are a regular thing."

The winds came regularly, ushering in a new cold front every week or so. My only nest-building activities so far had been buying a couple of potted succulents. One container was large and heavy enough I didn't worry about wind damage. I brought the smaller Kalanchoe inside the rig for protection each time strong winds blew our way, not wanting to find it on the other side of the park.

"I remember now how much work gardening is," I said to Michael. "I don't want to have to worry about bringing a plant in and out, wondering what will happen to it when we run into town to pick up our groceries."

"There you go," my husband said. "Just another reason why you should be grateful I bought you an RV."

I made a face at him.

We zipped along Dillon Road, heading back to the RV park after a grocery store run in Palm Springs. The landscape almost always made me gasp at its beauty and starkness—sand, rocks, and scrubby desert foliage on either side, huge mountains off in the distance in every direction.

But on this trip back home, I saw something different, and it wasn't pretty.

"This place looks like a huge garbage dump," I said. "Think they're trying to create a landfill or something?"

Michael, sitting in the passenger seat, looked out the window. "You're right. There's garbage everywhere. Looks like it's mostly plastic stuff."

"I wouldn't think people would throw that much litter out their car windows. No one does that anymore."

"Kids do when their parents aren't watching," Michael said.

"All this garbage makes the place look poor. Even the nice middle-class houses look junky with garbage strewn around."

"They probably pick it up every day. Guess more just keeps blowing in." Michael shrugged.

I watched as the wind picked up an empty plastic bag and blew it ten feet from where it'd been lying. Another thought occurred to me.

"You know, with the lack of rain and such low humidity, there's nothing out here that'd ever make this stuff disintegrate. All this plastic is going to be here for centuries."

"Yeah, I guess. Unless someone comes out here and picks it up."

"Some of it you'd almost have to chase down." I remembered plastic bags and small, lightweight items that blew across our campground. The base of the chain-link fence surrounding the park was several inches deep with accumulated trash trapped by the fence, anything from fast food wrappers to empty water bottles to small, unidentifiable plastic lids. "Maybe it didn't even come from passing motorists. Maybe it blows out of garbage cans, and maybe this entire desert is filled with a constant reshuffling of garbage by the wind from one place to another."

"Well, it'll all eventually end up in Arizona or Nevada," my husband said. "The winds always come from the west, so all this trash is moving to the east."

There he goes again, I thought, always trying to show me how smart he is. I'd have thought of that, too, if it weren't for these damn masks making me stupid.

However, I'd later learn my brilliant husband had it both right and wrong this time around, and so did I. Some of those winds did indeed have their origins in the Pacific Ocean. However, others reached the Great Basin via thermals from the Arctic, and those winds blew west toward us and the Pacific Ocean.

Also, as we'd later realize, those winds did a lot more than bring cold fronts and rearrange garbage. They also brought wildfires. By Thanksgiving, we'd find ourselves terrified of winds like these.

Another kind of blowing in the wind had occurred to me since meeting the Xscapers. In some ways, these nomads were like drifters. It was easy to view them as blowing in the wind, going here and there, no particular destination. They were not about getting anywhere in particular. They were about living with wheels under their houses. They probably didn't even think about where they were half the time.

I remembered Michael's dogged determination during our first few years of RV travel to go to every state in the United States. We'd bought a sticker map, and my driven, obsessed husband became intent on filling in every one of those states except Hawaii. He rejoiced when we completed the final ones in 2019. Although missing Hawaii, we'd picked up stickers for five Canadian Provinces, which more than compensated for not having Hawaii, in my opinion.

As we'd walk through our Xscaper neighborhood in the RV park, I'd see an occasional sticker map. I never saw a map with more than a dozen or so stickers. The states filled in were primarily in the west, sparsely populated places like Utah, Wyoming, Montana, and Idaho. Some of these folks had been full-timers a decade or more. Obviously, bragging rights of how many states they'd been to wasn't important to them. Those maps reminded me of the adage: It's about the journey, not the destination.

I understood myself well enough to know I was a driven, Type A personality who needed goals and projects. I spent three to five hours a day sitting at my laptop, either writing or editing. I wondered if I would ever be able to stop working and just be. Somehow, I didn't think so. I'd probably work myself to death. But could I ever blow in the wind as some of these fellow RVers seemed to be doing?

I realized how fortunate I was that my choice of 'work' didn't depend on a fixed address. Maybe I should start thinking of Michael and myself as blowing in the wind, just as I viewed the Xscapers. Had we finally found our tribe? Maybe.

If one goes online and looks up "blow" in the Urban Dictionary, several unusual definitions, references, and usages appear. Some are funny; others are crude. My frequent slang usage of "blow" refers to items or situations that are unpleasant, i.e., they suck.

In thinking about Bob Dylan's song and RVing, I realized there were possibly RVers, former and current, who found bouncing around in a tin can house to be a lifestyle that blows. We'd spent enough time in RV parks to understand that not all folks living in such small cramped quarters did it voluntarily. We'd seen more than a handful of substandard, un-roadworthy RVs with large families cramped inside because the residents couldn't afford anything better. Many of these RVs wouldn't bounce even if their residents wanted them to. I'd also read of elderly people living in deteriorated RVs, searching for back alleys and side streets to park overnight because they couldn't afford to pay park fees.

I understood our middle-class RVing experiences landed us squarely in the category of lucky people who could afford a retirement of ease and comfort. We RVed because we wanted to, not because we couldn't afford other choices.

We knew someone from back home who hated RVing, and she'd never even tried it. Her name was Betty, and she worked as a receptionist in our doctor's office in Tampa. Michael and I had gone to this office for thirty years and knew every employee on a first-name basis. When we first bought an RV and Michael told the office staff, Betty expressed horror. She said her husband talked of doing this, and she wasn't interested one bit. Two years later, she reported that her recently retired husband had just bought a travel trailer, which he intended to live in during hunting and fishing trips. "He wants me to go with him, and I'm not doing it. I want no part of that damned thing."

"That's an interesting story," I said to Michael later. "I wonder how that'll work out." The conversation took place a couple of years ago. The last we heard, Betty's husband went off on his hunting and fishing trips, and Betty stayed home.

"I'm glad I didn't pull a Betty," I later said to Michael. While I'd started the adventure with resistance that sometimes bordered on angst, my overwhelming feelings had been positive, even from the beginning. I'd appreciated and valued the new experiences and insights. Plus, I'd found a unique voice and a new topic for writing.

For me, this feeling of blowing in the wind, untethered and free, felt dreamy and wonderful. While I'd initially been reluctant, I'd tried it and gradually came to embrace it. As I often found myself doing these days, I shook my head in awe that it had taken a pandemic to make me finally go full-time in this thing.

CHAPTER 24

IS ANYTHING SAFE ANYMORE?

Just because we cocooned in our RV during the coronavirus pandemic, life was not always easy, and our best options were not always easy to identify. We found ourselves in a world where it appeared as if common sense had died.

"The CDC guidelines are perfectly clear," my Covid-obsessed husband said one morning, authority in his voice. He'd just finished his predictable two-hour daily reading of newspapers. His voice quivered with anger and agitation. "All people have to do, dammit, is wear masks, distance themselves from other people, and stay home unless they have to buy groceries or pick up prescriptions." He sloshed coffee on the table as he slammed his mug down with a thud.

I paused at my laptop, my hands hovering a couple of inches above the keys. "What's ticked you off this time?"

"Just read about this Covid party some college kids threw. They got together and breathed on each other for several hours, thinking they'd prove the virus was a hoax. Now five of them are sick, one in the hospital. How stupid can you get?"

"That sounds pretty bad, but before you get too much more upset, maybe you should remember that we've taken unnecessary chances, too."

"What are you talking about? We don't take chances."

"Oh, yeah? What about our little excursion down Sunrise Way two days ago, stopping at Tommy Bahamas for drinks and chips? Was that essential?" I knew we took unnecessary risks sometimes, but how could we not lapse occasionally? We'd decided we had to stop risking those afternoon drinks, even when they were outside like Tommy Bahama's had been. But because we were so starved to do something normal and fun, we'd given in. I knew I had pandemic fatigue, was sick of all the restrictions, just like millions of other Americans. Sometimes one had to take a risk to keep from going crazy, I thought, though I knew I was lying to myself.

"That was not particularly risky," Michael said. "We were ten feet away from the closest other customers, and the place did not have those misters spraying water particles all over the place."

We had wondered about the sidewalk misters in front of restaurants as we'd walked down that popular restaurant-lined street in Palm Springs. "Don't those things look dangerous, like they could be spreading virus particles right in people's faces?" I'd asked.

"Hmmm," Michael said, "you could be right. You know why they're here, though, right?"

"Of course. To help cool people off from the brutal heat." While our stroll took place in November, with temperatures hovering in the mid-80s, temperatures during the summer months in Palm Springs could reach 130 degrees. I'd come with Michael to this area many years ago during July for a national sales meeting with his company. It was the first time I'd seen sidewalk misters, and they'd left an impression. I came from Florida, and summer humidity generally stayed around 85%. I'd never been to a climate where anyone would add more humidity, although I understood the primary reason for the mist was cooling.

My question intrigued my husband. As we paid our tab, Michael asked our waitress about the misters and whether they spread germs. She didn't know, so Michael asked to speak with the manager to ask the same question. The manager didn't have an answer either, shrugging his shoulders and saying, "We all get inspected regularly by State officials, and they've never questioned the safety of misters, as far as I know."

As we left Tommy Bahama's, we passed a couple of uniformed paramedics on the sidewalk. Michael did an about-face and asked them about the misters and their potential for spreading coronavirus particles in the air. The two young men acted surprised at the question. They didn't have an answer, with one saying, "Never thought about it, and I haven't a clue."

A couple of weeks later, Michael read a new research study that found humidity lowered infection risk. The coronavirus particles would attach to water molecules, and the weight would make them sink to the floor rather than hover in the air. Looking back, we might have enjoyed our Tommy Bahama drinks at one of the most dangerous sidewalk cafes in Palm Springs.

As our fears of catching Covid-19 increased, we began to pay more attention to what our fellow Xscapers did in our secluded section of this Desert Hot Springs RV oasis.

"Listen to this," Michael said. "Someone here just posted on Facebook that the aerial tramway in Downtown Palm Springs is open. She went up in it today, said it was great." He paused. "Have you looked at the photographs of those cable cars online? They're all enclosed, eighty people all crammed into this little thing for a ten-minute ride up the mountain."

"They're probably limiting the number of people in each car now because of Covid," I said. "Plus, I think they can open the windows for better ventilation." I'd seen the pictures online. The spinning cable cars went up over two-and-a-half miles to Mt. San Jacinto State Park, an almost vertical ascent that offered views of the Chino Canyon cliffs. The temperature at the top was about 30-40 degrees cooler than at the base. I'd almost be willing to risk infection to take that tramway ride up to the top. It looked like a great trip.

"I don't care. It was an unnecessary risk," Michael said.

"Not as bad as the neighbors next door who went for pedicures."

"They did what?" Michael asked, a bit of hysteria in his voice.

"They got pedicures. But is that any worse than us getting haircuts in Leadville a couple of months ago?" I asked.

"The pandemic wasn't nearly as out of control back then."

"You're splitting hairs, no pun intended." I laughed. "What about our trip to Bed Bath & Beyond the other day?"

"That was essential. Our coffeemaker stopped working." Michael's voice was slightly higher, and I realized we were getting into a potentially volatile area.

"We could have ordered online and opted for curbside delivery."

"I wanted to make sure we got one we liked," Michael said. "I didn't want some teenager picking out a coffeemaker for us. We learned our lesson about teenaged shoppers with online grocery shopping."

I realized we all took our little chances, justifying and rationalizing whatever we did. I'd gone to a Home Depot gardening center a few days earlier and bought a couple of succulents. Why? I felt down and knew plants would cheer me up. I risked the outing, telling myself the garden shop was outside in the open air, and there'd be no risk at all. I wondered how our neighbors had felt about me coming home with plants. Would they have viewed my outing to a garden shop as essential?

We told ourselves grocery stores were safe as long as everyone wore masks. We both felt the angst of not stocking up on items to reduce the frequency of our shopping trips. Our RV was too small and lacked the storage space to buy duplicates or stock up. At least we tried to minimize the amount of time we spent in the supermarket each time by splitting our grocery list in two, with each of us taking half. However, throw in all the impulsive purchases we made—and we were both guilty of this— we'd invariably end up with almost more food than our small refrigerator would hold. Sometimes we had to leave paper goods and nonperishables in the back of the car until we had room for them inside.

We wanted to develop a few friendships among these Xscapers, so we tried to figure out who in our group followed Covid protocols similar to ours. Our strategy would then be to give a wide berth to those neighbors we thought might pose more risk to us. Folks came and went from the park, just as Michael and I did, but we had no way of knowing where they went or what they did.

It was easier to figure out with the outdoor lovers. In our group, we had a couple of avid rock climbers, and they had offered to teach the sport to others in our group. They'd post photos on the group's Facebook page of them with another couple, usually climbing in Joshua Tree National Park. We knew they rode in separate cars to the park. They were socially distanced and outside in every photo. Our group also contained professional photographers, enthusiastic birders, and dedicated hikers and walkers. They all seemed to spend a lot of time in the many canyons and preserves in the area. These activities seemed safe to us.

I suspected almost everyone in the group except us frequented the four hot mineral springs in the park. The springs opened at 9:00 A.M. every morning and closed at 10:00 P.M. every night. We'd see folks wearing robes and carrying towels walking back and forth from the office/pool area. The park also had a large heated swimming pool and a hot tube large enough for at least twenty people.

When we'd decided to come to this RV park for the winter, I'd imagined soaking a few minutes in one of the park's mineral hot springs every day. I even ordered waffle-weave robes from Amazon for Michael and me to wear over our bathing suits.

I managed to talk Michael into one visit to the hot springs area, and he freaked out. Although management limited the number of people in each of the four mineral springs to four at a time, the springs were small and 6-ft. socially distancing was not possible. In addition, management did not require masks in the springs, and we never saw anyone wearing one. When we'd ask about it, folks gave us incredulous looks and answers, as if masks in the water were the most ridiculous idea in the world. We resisted mentioning that our first public pandemic swimming experiences had been in a nudist RV park where masks were mandatory. We, too, might have viewed wearing a mask in the water as absurd had it not been for our experiences in south Texas.

Maybe somewhere down the road, Michael will find another time and place to wear his new waffle-weave robe. He made it clear it wouldn't be at a mineral hot spring during a pandemic.

Almost half of the Xscapers in this Winter Home Base group were solo travelers. It seemed their needs for connection and social interactions with others were more significant than for old married couples like Michael and me. I couldn't hide my outrage (although I contained it within our RV) when one of these younger solo RVers invited folks to meet at the hot tub at 7:30 each evening, and at least six people said yes.

We had a lot more trouble figuring out the level of caution our neighbors took concerning shopping. Michael and I had become Amazon shopping fanatics. We tried to do most of our grocery shopping online and would take delivery in the store's parking lot. We saw many of our neighbors returning to their rigs with Amazon boxes retrieved from the park office. Occasionally we'd see a Walmart delivery service drop off groceries at one of our hosts' rigs. But for the most part, almost everyone seemed to do their food shopping in person inside stores. We were surprised and somewhat dismayed by this observation, despite understanding too well the problems with online shopping.

We saw a few in our group who seemed to shop in stores every day, with trips to Home Depot, Trader Joe's, Total Wine & More, Bed Bath & Beyond, specialty meat markets, upscale grocery stores, and more. Granted, Michael and I occasionally ran into stores like these, too, but we curbed our enthusiasm big-time as the pandemic escalated. These shopping excursions seemed incredibly unsafe and unnecessary to us.

The pandemic surged, and Thanksgiving brought staggering increases in Covid-19 cases. CDC predictions for the holiday season were dire, and I wondered if anyone would survive. When I realized my paranoia had mushroomed out of control, I focused on becoming more tolerant and accepting of my new RVing friends and neighbors' behaviors. For the first time, I began to realize our new friends' perceptions of our choices might seem as perplexing as our understandings of theirs.

"You know, Michael, our behaviors at these Xscaper happy hours get as out-of-control as the next person's. It's just like those happy hours down in the Rio Grande Valley. The more people drink, the closer they get, the louder their voices become, and the more likely the masks will drop below the chins. Come on now. It's time that we get over our sanctimonious attitudes and realize we're doing no better and no worse than anyone else."

"But vaccines are right around the corner," my husband said. "We can't give up now, not when there's a promise it'll all end before long."

I sighed. He was right. We'd lived with our fears and anxieties for nine months already. We could probably continue for another six months until the country was safer.

"Well, you're probably right, but I am so weary of this pandemic."

"Don't worry, Little Cherrie. It'll all be over before you know it."

Again, I muttered 'jerk' under my breath. This time I added 'liar' to the unspoken dialogue. I didn't for a minute believe I wouldn't feel every damn second of the rest of this scourge. And not just until it was over. I'd remember it for the rest of my life, just as I'm sure every other person on the planet would.

I also realized I'd remember every one of these Xscapers with whom we now shared this pandemic, whether I thought they were making good choices or not. There was nothing stronger than shared anxiety to facilitate bonding. It almost made me trust every single one of them.

The Xscaper hosts had told us at the first happy hour gathering of the group: "You will become like family." I realized they were right. And in families, members often disagreed. Maybe not everything had to be safe to feel okay.

CHAPTER 25

THANKSGIVING BLOWS IN

The infamous Santa Ana winds, or perhaps I should call them gales, increased their ferocity ten-fold on Thanksgiving Eve. They were strong, dry, down-sloped winds that originated in the Great Basin. The Great Basin included most of Nevada, half of Utah, and sections of Idaho, Wyoming, Oregon, and California. Meteorologists in the western United States west refer to the Santa Ana as 'devil winds,' and for excellent reason. They trigger wildfires.

We sat in our cozy motorhome, Michael watching the evening news while I considered starting dinner and ruminated about the 3-lb. turkey breast we planned to cook on our Weber-Q grill for our Thanksgiving dinner. Michael hadn't wanted the turkey breast. He'd wanted a prime Ribeye steak.

"But it's Thanksgiving," I'd said. Now I second-guessed buying that traditional holiday fowl. I vowed, however, to do everything possible to make that turkey melt-in-your-mouth tender and juicy. Otherwise, I'd feel guilty.

"Wow, wait 'til you hear this." Michael's volume and voice reflected excitement. "This area is under a Red Alert for both power outages and wildfires. We could spend Thanksgiving Day and Friday without power. Or worse yet, running for our lives from a wildfire."

This terrifying news report scared the bejesus out of me. "Why do you sound so friggin' excited? I think we should pack up and leave right now."

"Calm down, Little Cherrie. You'll be okay." He shot me a grin. I shot him a bird.

Later that night, fellow Xscapers in the park began making Facebook posts on the group's private page. "The high wind warning is calling for gusts up to 65-75 mph. Better batten down the hatches!"

It was late, and I didn't see the post until the next morning. I didn't need to see the post when I woke up to know the winds blew strong. The wind picked up progressively as Thanksgiving Day progressed. By noon, we'd stashed all the folding chairs under the rig, rolled up the outside mat and wedged in partway under a front tire, and moved the grill as close to the rig as possible. I safely tucked my two beautiful pots of succulents inside the coach behind the driver's seat. All our neighbors were taking similar actions to secure anything the wind might lift and deposit elsewhere.

"Well, we're obviously not going to be cooking that turkey breast outside today," Michael said.

"And if we lose our power, we might be either eating it raw or having peanut butter and jelly sandwiches for Thanksgiving dinner."

"Not so, Little Cherrie. You forget we have a generator. We'll do just fine. Don't you worry your little head about anything."

"What about the propane? Isn't the gauge almost on empty? We should have gone yesterday and filled up the tank."

"Would you just calm down?"

"My mamma always told me I was born to fret and stew." My husband was making me mad, and my obsession over that damn turkey breast was making me a bit unhinged. "Guess this'll be a Thanksgiving to remember, huh?"

It was a Thanksgiving to remember. The Santa Ana winds howled nonstop for two days. While we saw occasional items blowing through

165

the campground, it didn't feel like the winds were stronger than 35-40 mph in our little section of the desert. Still, I felt happy not to see any small dogs blowing around. These winds were plenty powerful enough to pump my adrenaline up a few notches.

Local news reported a few rolling blackouts in the area, but our power stayed on. At first, I wasn't sure about the connection between strong winds and loss of power. I learned from local meteorologists that gusts took down power lines, power lines triggered sparks, and sparks started the wildfires. Well, duh! How would I have known this? I was a Florida girl, and our wildfires were usually started by lightning, a cigarette thrown out a car window, or arson.

The desert was dry, and little could burn, other than houses and other buildings. I looked out across the sandy, rocky terrain and saw only occasional bone-dry, brittle shrubs dotting the landscape. While the rainy season in this desert lasted from November through March each year, we'd not seen a drop of rain in the almost four weeks we'd been here. Even if some rain had fallen, it wouldn't have helped much. This area received only about 5" of rain in an entire year. But with Global Warming, who knew what it'd be from now on.

Nothing other than our menu felt traditional about this Thanksgiving Day. The Xscapers discouraged pot luck meals, or we might have shared a meal outside at a picnic table with our next-door neighbors. I suppose we could have made those arrangements, but we didn't, and neither did any of the other couples at our end of the park. It would have been hard to eat outside in this kind of wind storm.

A group of solo RVers at the other end did make social plans. They ate their Thanksgiving dinners together, 2-ft. apart at a picnic table. Michael and I walked down in the late afternoon to say hello. They'd all prepared their meals independently and simply arrived at the table at the agreed-upon time to eat together. We noted they had to carefully hang on to their plates lest the Santa Ana gusts blow their dinners away.

It broke my heart to remember we'd made plans three months earlier to join RVing friends—Craig, Arline, Bill, and Diane—for Thanksgiving at this park. We'd met them in Taos back in June and had stayed in touch. They had arrived on Wednesday and had reservations to stay for five days. The plan had been for us to join them for a potluck Thanksgiving dinner.

Michael and I canceled out the potluck dinner about a week before the holiday. While we would have felt safe—we knew these people well enough to know they'd lived as cautiously as we had—we decided it'd be unfair to risk it because of the Xscapers' request that there be no potlucks. We would have felt awful if we'd been the ones to introduce Covid-19 into our group.

Meanwhile, I couldn't find words to express my chagrin on Thanksgiving afternoon. I'd canceled out with our friends because of the Xscapers' policy of no potlucks, only to see members of the Xscapers huddled together eating their Thanksgiving dinners two feet apart.

Maybe I needed to learn to bend the rules once in a while.

"It'll have to be inside for our turkey breast," Michael said. It was about 5:00 P.M., time to think about getting our dinner started. Outside, darkness had fallen, and temperatures had dropped to the upper fifties. The Santa Ana winds still raged.

"I think we could do it in the oven," I said.

"No, I don't think the heat gets high enough or is that consistent. I'll cook it in the toaster oven."

"So, you're going to do it?" I asked. "It just looks too big to fit in there, like it'd burn on the top being so close to the burners." I'd have thought that it'd be up to me to figure it out given how much he didn't want the thing. I should have realized my cooking-fool hubby, who viewed himself as a yet-undiscovered master gourmet chef, would want the honors of cooking the holiday entree.

"Look at this." Michael had taken the turkey out of its vacuum-packed wrapper and had found a plastic pouch of gravy base resting on top of the meat. Without that pouch and the plastic wrap, the breast collapsed a bit and perfectly fit on the toaster oven baking sheet. The rest of our humble meal consisted of dressing, roasted broccoli, and cranberry sauce.

Later, our stomachs stuffed and the kitchen cleaned, Michael admitted the dinner exceeded his expectations. Given that the entree was turkey, I accepted his assessment without comment.

"You know, I'm really put out about today," I said to Michael later that night as we were buckling down for the evening. The winds outside were so strong we could feel the motorhome sway. "I'm thinking about those folks down there at the other end of the park. They were all squeezed together, eating and drinking and laughing, no masks on their faces and less than 2-ft. apart. I am so sorry we didn't join our Taos friends for that potluck Thanksgiving dinner."

"Hey, we can't second-guess," Michael said, "not when the promise of a vaccine is so close. We're pandemic weary, just like everyone else. But this is not the time to let our guard down. We did the right thing."

I lay in bed a long time that night before falling asleep. We'd had a good day. We'd visited and shared a few drinks with our Taos friends in the afternoon before they had their holiday meal. We'd chatted with several neighbors and then stopped by to say hello to eight or nine of our group at the other end of the park. We'd talked with my daughter Kate, who'd attended a gathering of seven people for Thanksgiving dinner. Then we'd chatted with Michael's sister in Connecticut, who shared Thanksgiving dinner inside a house with ten people. The most satisfying visit had been on the telephone with our best friends in Tampa, who, like us, eschewed family, friends, and neighbors for an at-home Thanksgiving dinner for two.

It felt as if those Santa Ana winds rocking the rig were trying to rock me to sleep. The wind soothed like the gurgling streams or the dripping raindrops on canned sleep tapes. I'd first felt the impact of this Covid-19 in my life in April when we'd become stranded in the Rio Grande Valley in south Texas. It was now the end of November, seven months later. Just because hunkering down now came almost naturally didn't mean I needed to like it.

So far, despite the discomfort of wearing a mask, the inconvenience of not popping into stores whenever the urge struck, and the anxieties of what the future would hold, I was doing okay. The pandemic had led me to sell the house in Tampa, and I'd not regretted that decision for a fleeting moment. My husband was ecstatic that we were finally full-time RVers. We were feeling happy, seeing gorgeous parts of the country we'd never seen before, making new friends at every stop, and spending significant amounts of time exercising in the fresh air and sunshine.

I finally drifted off to sleep with the thought that this might be the happiest and most relaxed I'd ever been in my life. Michael was right. We had to maintain our discipline by following CDC guidelines to the letter. Otherwise, we might never see another Thanksgiving.

And mixed in with those happy feelings about the choices we'd made concerning this Thanksgiving Day, I confess to a bit of self-righteousness. I couldn't help but think everyone we knew had taken more risks on this holiday than we had. What does one do with a little feeling of self-pity other than trying to find a way to feel sanctimonious?

CHAPTER 26

HEALTHY SOLITUDE?

After a month of hunkering down in a desert RV park with nineteen other rigs, my thoughts about social relationships began to change. Again.

More than thirty years ago, I read a book called *Solitude: A Return to the Self.* In the book, published in 1988, psychiatrist Anthony Storr posited a hypothesis that contradicted current thinking. Mental health professionals generally believed there was a positive relationship between the ability to get along well with others and high scores on mental health scales. Storr, in contrast, maintained that getting along with oneself was just as important, if not more important, than how one functioned with others. His premise challenged the mainstream belief that participation in groups and intimate social relationships brought happiness (and excellent mental health).

When first published, Storr's theory sounded radical, almost heretical, to psychological thought. My mental health colleagues reacted in horror when I excitedly raved about this new way of viewing mental health. I was just a social worker, after all, not a psychologist or a psychiatrist.

I found Storr's formulation titillating and invigorating. He verbalized a thought that'd been percolating below my conscious level for a while. Storr made it sound healthy to want to be alone, to want to work independently rather than in groups, and not to want to spend all one's waking time with other people. Just reading Storr's book improved my mental health by several notches, or so I thought. Finally, someone had iterated what my psyche felt to be true.

In time, I stashed the book on a crowded shelf and moved on to other ideas. Storr's theory appeared to have had little impact on the mental health community. I hadn't thought about Anthony Storr again for decades until we joined the Xscapers for a Winter Home Base shelter from the Covid-19 storm.

"Jeez, Michael, can you believe these folks who go out in the desert, or wherever they go, and stay there for weeks on end, never seeing or talking to another soul?"

"Well, they probably talk to others online, on video or Zoom, or something like that. Most of them work full-time, after all."

"But think of someone like Jenny, RVing alone with a couple of dogs, and those dogs certainly don't look like they'd provide any protection. I was talking to her the other day," I said. "She told me she loved being out there by herself, that she never got scared. If it were me, I'd start hearing things that went 'bump in the night' the minute the sun went down."

"But you're a psycho," my husband said. "You jump three feet off the ground and scream if I walk up unexpectedly behind you in a room."

"Comes from living in large, crime-infested metropolitan areas for the past fifty years."

"Most people aren't so easily startled," Michael said.

"Well, most people haven't knocked on doors making home visits the way I did as a social worker. I probably have a better handle on how many violent, crazy people are out there and how irrational and mean they can get when strung out on drugs."

I didn't feel like giving my forty-five-minute spiel of some of the crazy stuff I'd seen, like the time I walked out of an inner-city apartment and found the building surrounded by a SWAT Team. My husband didn't want to hear it again. Still, I thought my experiences explained my spookiness perfectly well.

A few minutes later, Michael said, "I think the folks in our group have spent most of their time out here in the west. It's sparsely populated, not like the east coast where crowding and crime are so rampant."

"I get the feeling they hate being in this RV park. It's like they can hardly wait to leave. Makes me wonder why they bothered to come here."

"I agree they're a standoffish group socially. Except for a couple of them, like Liza next door—my God, isn't she like a social butterfly flitting all over? —most of them seem to stay inside their rigs all day, hardly even sticking their noses out the door for fresh air." We'd become friendly with our next-door neighbors, Liza Simpson and Chris Wickland. I was surprised to hear Michael describing Liza that way. It sounded more like something I might have said. It crossed my mind that maybe my husband and I'd had far too much togetherness during the past nine months.

Michael made his harrumph sound of impatience and said, "These people around here are working, and you're overthinking everything. Give it a break."

"Well, the couple of folks on the other side of us are hermits if I've ever seen hermits. I haven't seen the woman since the day they backed that big Class A into the site, and except for a trip somewhere in the car about once a week, the only time I see the guy is when he opens the door in the mornings to let that little Chihuahua out."

"Brad seems to think they don't socialize because the guy can't hear what anyone says. He said he'd tried to talk to him one time, had shouted, and the guy still couldn't make out what he was saying." Brad was a friend across the street in the park.

"That's a sad story," I said, "and come to think of it, I think that woman used a walker when she finally got up from the passenger seat when they first arrived. But that's different from the sense I get with all these other Xscapers. They almost seem to go out of their way to avoid running into anyone else."

"They certainly turn out in force for the scheduled happy hours, though, don't they?"

"Point taken," I said. "They do like to drink." I paused. A couple of minutes later, "Think you and I are both going to be alcoholics before this coronavirus thing is over? Not much else to look forward to at the end of the day other than a couple of glasses of red wine."

"For you, three or four might be more accurate."

"Not funny. I'm not talking to you anymore. Maybe I'll pour myself a glass of wine instead." This time I rolled my eyes at him.

As time went on and I added more information to my observations and impressions of my fellow RVers, I became more intrigued. They felt like a different breed of RVer than I'd encountered before. They were living in RVs as opposed to traveling, touring, or vacationing. These folks seemed to have nothing in common with the snowbirds who routinely opted for seasonal resorts with social activities and friends to connect with on a regular basis. Or even with the full-time RVers who planned itineraries around holidays and significant occasions with family members and friends spread all over the country. All the full-timers we'd met up until now had been gregarious, out-going, and welcoming of chit-chat, happy hour invitations, and spontaneous get-togethers. I had to consider, however, that Covid-19 could well have been a factor in the current behaviors of our neighbors. Without a pandemic raging, they might have been knocking on my door nine times a day.

While gardening had been a solitary pursuit for me during my previous life of sticks-and-bricks living, I'd managed to turn that into a social event by becoming a Master Gardener. While writing was a lonely, isolated activity, I'd turned this into a social network via critique and writing group meetings. Reading books morphed into get-togethers in the form of book clubs. Even bicycling became social with occasional rides with friends. Had I been a social butterfly myself back in my former life?

The longer we hung out in Desert Hot Springs with the Xscapers, the more comfortable I felt. It was as if I was returning to the person I was meant to be. Self-contained. Self-reliant. Independent of the opinions of others. Free to explore, to test, to experiment. I felt freer than I'd felt in decades. Was I ready to go out on Bureau of Land Management (BLM) land for weeks on end? Well, maybe I wasn't prepared to go that far. I could only hope my social skills wouldn't disappear from disuse. But hot damn, it felt good!

We'd been meeting every couple of weeks on Zoom with our RVillage Rally friends, Jack and Naydne Huber. I asked him one time about the value of our RVillage membership. This virtual community had an option to post our whereabouts online. And then, RVillage would electronically notify us when another RVillage member arrived in our area. I'd signed up for this notification, thinking it'd be a good way of meeting other RVers as we traveled.

"Jack," I said during one of our virtual happy hours. "Every time we move, I update our location on RVillage. I almost always get several notifications of other RVers in our area, sometimes even in the same RV park we're in. But nothing ever comes of it, even when I send a quick email saying 'hi, we're in site such and such, drop by and say hello.' What's the point of it all if no one ever responds?"

"It's the pandemic," Jack said. "Everyone's afraid now."

"Yeah," Nadyne added. "It used to be we'd pull into a new park, stick our RVillage herald flag in the ground, and within the next hour or so, we'd have three or four couples drop by. Not anymore. People are staying to themselves."

"Wait until Covid-19 clears up. Things will return to the way they used to be, and you'll meet more people than you ever wanted to know," Jack said.

I thought a lot about the Hubers' report. Perhaps it would indeed work out that way, but I wasn't ready yet to make any bets on it. It felt like this pandemic had maybe traumatized me too much, somehow leaving me with a permanent, indelible wariness of others. But was this fallout from the coronavirus? Maybe, instead, might it be a deeper level of understanding of who and what I really was?

This pandemic had created an entire world of socially-distanced people, many of whom now lived in solitude or close to it. How many might discover it felt better, and more natural, to live distanced from others? While the fear of contracting Covid-19 could well be driving the Xscapers in this RV oasis in Desert Hot Springs to keep to themselves, I believed most of them had discovered the truth of Anthony Storr's message, whether they'd ever heard of his book or not. I knew I had.

CHAPTER 27

DESERT CHARMS

Some folks adore the desert—the starkness, the harshness, and the emptiness. I began to view many of our Xscaper neighbors as bona fide desert rats, folks who felt most at home out on the open range, in the wilderness, far away from civilization and other people.

The term 'desert rat' should not be confused with real desert rats, however. I was horrified when I learned a real rat had invaded one of the rigs in our group, established residency, and refused to leave. Well, maybe it was a mouse, not a rat. Still, who wants a rodent scurrying around—scratch, scratch, scratching—at 3:00 A.M. every night? It might not have been quite so bad if her dog hadn't gone berserk with the noise, waking up folks in all the surrounding rigs. Luckily, our rig was far enough away that we never heard the commotion.

I couldn't shake the image of mice, or other varmints, invading our rig. At least a couple of times a day, I'd say to Michael, "What if we get mice, or rats, or a snake? There's got to be something we could do, don't you think?"

"Stop being such a psycho," my unconcerned spouse said.

About a week later, as we sat outside drinking beer and wine with our next-door neighbors during one of our regular happy hours, I asked Chris, "Do you worry about rodents getting in your rig?"

"Nope," he said. "I ordered these plugins from Amazon. They emit a high-frequency noise that we can't hear—Maggie can't hear it either—and it's supposed to keep out any kind of animal." Maggie was their dog.

"Wow. Michael, we need those things, like today," I said.

I asked Chris for more specific information, and he went to his rig and returned with one of the plugins in his hand. It was a white, egg-shaped, palm-sized plastic device with the name Ever Pest printed on it.

"They look like nightlights when plugged in," Liza said. "We keep two going all the time, one at each end of the rig."

"And they work?" I asked.

"I guess," Chris said. "We haven't seen or heard any signs of an infestation."

The next day, I went on Amazon and found the Ever Pests, along with dozens of other similar devices for pest control. Amazon advertised these high-frequency emitting devices for every kind of building or situation imaginable, not just for RVs. At $11.99 each, I ordered two. When they arrived, I was amazed to read they were supposedly effective against roaches, ants, flies, and mosquitos in addition to small mammals like mice and rats. This new information made me sorry I hadn't had these devices plugged into every room in our house in Tampa.

I noted with disappointment, however, that the Ever Pest flyer made no mention of snakes.

When our Taos friends from Riverside, California, came to see us over Thanksgiving weekend, Diane said, "You know, there's something very Zen about the desert. We've only been here two days, and already my blood pressure has dropped."

"Yes, it's very relaxing, in a way that's hard to describe," Arline said.

"I hadn't thought about it before," I said, "but I think you're right. I realized a few days ago that, for the first time in years, I'm having really good dreams at night. Before we got here, when I'd sometimes remember a dream, it was usually almost like a nightmare."

"You're sleeping better," Arline said. "The desert does that for you."

I'd think about this conversation many times in the next few days. Here we were, living during a pandemic that could take our lives at any time, trapped in a cheap-ass RV park in the middle of the desert, far from family, friends, and everything that was known and familiar, with only a cracker box house on wheels to call home. This reality did not fit at all with the realization that I felt more relaxed and calmer than I'd felt for years. Maybe Diane was right. Perhaps this desert contained a Zen that was realigning my chakras.

A favorite pastime for our Xscaper Home Basers seemed to be taking long hikes in the desert.

"We really ought to do that," I said to Michael one morning. "We've been here for several weeks already. We need to get out, get some exercise and fresh air."

"We're still settling in. Don't rush things."

Yeah, right. It takes about thirty minutes to set up a rig and settle in. I understood Michael's reluctance, however. It looked hot and harsh out there on this valley floor.

Group activities among the Xscapers began around 4:00 P.M. each day, most often with a happy hour to watch the sunset. The sun dropping behind the San Jacinto Mountains to the west created some of the most breathtaking palettes of color I'd ever seen in my life.

But before I'd let any of these West Coasters lay claim to the best sunsets in the world, I'd have to mention my roots. I'd put a sunset on the horizon of the Gulf of Mexico, viewed from an upstairs balcony bar at the Hurricane Seafood Restaurant in Pass-s-Grille, Florida, next to this desert sunset any day of the week. The ones out here are like a rainbow—purples, reds, pinks, oranges, golds, and yellows. The ones on the Gulf, in contrast, begin as pure brilliant gold and then gradually dissolve into those other colors. We didn't have the mountains in Florida, but we saw double sunsets in the water's reflection.

The Xscaper happy hours generally ended around 5:30. Temperatures dropped quickly once the sun went down. Unless one had a propane fire pit to huddle around, it'd be too cold to stay outside. I found most of these Xscapers more tolerant of the cold than I was. I couldn't decide whether I thought my thin Florida blood just hadn't thickened up yet or whether it had to do with my senior status in the group. Of the thirty or so people in our group, only a couple were older than I.

Michael discovered yet another world in the desert when darkness fell. He'd often go out at ten or eleven at night and gaze at the sky. "Hey, Little Cherrie," he'd call. "Come look at this. Tonight, I can see Orion the Hunter, Pisces, and Cancer. And for planets, I can see Mars, Jupiter, Venus, and Saturn. I can't believe this. You've got to come look."

"Too cold," I'd yell from inside. "How can you stand it out there?"

"How can you ignore a sky like this? I've never seen so many stars in my life."

"I'll come out tomorrow," I said.

"Yeah, right." I could hear my husband muttering under his breath.

A few days later, I asked, "Have you seen the Big and Little Dippers? You haven't mentioned those."

"No, we must be too close to Los Angeles and the lights." Los Angeles was only a hundred miles away.

After another week of nagging and begging, I finally convinced Michael we should go hiking. I'd watched our neighbors don their sunhats and slather themselves with sunscreen often enough to think there must be something of interest out there that kept drawing them back.

"Maybe we'll find peace in the desert, maybe even enlightenment. We'll be like Carlos Castaneda, you know, with his Don Juan books. We'll see things, feel things, have insights into the meaning of life."

"I'll go if you provide the peyote," Michael said.

"Right. Dream on."

We googled hiking trails near Palm Springs and came up with many choices. We hiked the Swiss Canyon Trail and the Kim Nicol Trail, and we can testify that they were hot, hard, and exhausting. We next checked out the Indian Canyons Nature Preserve, private land on the Agua Caliente Indian Reservation. The Indian Canyons promised shady hikes through a palm tree oasis. We did indeed find lovely trails along gurgling streams. Huge native palm trees, locally known as elephant palms, lined the banks. Canyon walls of boulders rose on either side. In some places, we had to squeeze between trees and rocks to get through. In other areas, we had to climb over boulders to pick up the trail again.

"Hey, how about that Coachella Valley Nature Preserve?" Michael asked. "It's closer than Indian Canyons, and it's also supposed to be an oasis with palm trees. Liza and Chris go there a lot, and Joe says it's his favorite place."

Since Michael proposed the outing, I wasn't about to say no. "Absolutely. Let's do it."

The first mile or so of the Nature Preserve Trail was shady, with giant palm trees growing with their feet in bodies of water at the base. Boardwalks and small bridges spanned occasional pools of water. Occasionally we'd hit a spot so shady and protected it looked like dusk had descended. We learned this natural crevice in the earth was the San Andreas Fault.

"No wonder Joe likes this," I said. "This is absolutely gorgeous."

My enchantment didn't last long, however. We hiked the area several times, taking a different trail each time leading out from the end of the shady oasis. Each course led to an equally hot and challenging trek through a flat desert floor with rocks and dry shrubby desert vegetation. Along every trail, with what seemed like only a few yards between each one, rangers had posted cute little rattlesnake warning signs.

"Never again," I yelled when I came upon the fourth or fifth sign. "I'm never coming out here again with all these snakes. If I die, I'd rather it be from Covid, not a stupid snake bite."

"Calm down, Little Cherrie. Even if a snake bit you, you wouldn't die. I'd get you to the hospital, and you'd be fine in a couple of weeks."

"Oh, yeah? And how are you going to get an ambulance? There's no friggin' cell phone service out here."

"You dodo. Look right over there," my husband said.

Sure enough, there was a major road with lots of traffic paralleling our path. It'd be easy to flag down a motorist for help. Although embarrassed at my lack of situational awareness, I was sick and tired of all these snake warnings. It was almost like being in Florida with all the alligator warnings.

Our new Xscaper friend Joe loved both hiking and star-gazing. He told us a story of combining his two passions. "You know Bennett Road beside the park? The other night, I decided to take a walk back there, see if I could see any wildlife."

Michael laughed. "I can't think of any desert wildlife I'd want to encounter in the dark."

"Well, I was hoping I'd maybe see just the red eyes of a coyote, off at a distance," Joe said. "I don't think coyotes attack. I think they'd just run away if they saw a person."

"There are certainly some beautiful skies out here at night," Michael said.

"Absolutely," Joe said. "So, I put on my warmest clothes, stuck my earbuds in my ears, cranked the music up as high as it'd go, and started walking down Bennett Road. Must have walked more than an hour."

"Did you see any wildlife?" I asked.

"No, but it was one of the most incredible experiences I've ever had, out there in the desert at night, all by myself, looking up at all those stars. It was positively magical."

Later, I asked Michael, "You think Joe smokes a lot of pot?"

Michael laughed. "Maybe. Who knows? He's a mystical sort of guy anyway."

"I didn't want to say anything when Joe was talking, but all I could think about when he was telling his story was the RV park where we'd stayed in Tucson that time. Remember the one? It had all those warnings posted all over the place not to go outside at night without a flashlight, that rattlesnakes came out at night to warm up on the warm asphalt." I felt anxious just remembering my terror at seeing those signs.

"You're such a psycho," Michael said. "What's with this snake phobia you have?"

"It's not a phobia. It's genuine, honest-to-God respect for venomous serpents. And others must have it, too, or there wouldn't be all these signs warning about rattlesnakes."

"You should tell Joe that story," my husband said. "It might cool his jets about wanting to see wildlife in the desert at night."

While we found this desert life enjoyable and relaxing, we were not doing much hiking out there, and I didn't see us changing our ways until the weather cooled down. The sun was too intense during the day, the trails were often sandy and hard to walk on, and the heat and aridity left us dehydrated no matter how much water we drink. And for reasons already mentioned, I certainly wouldn't consider going out hiking at night.

That notion of walking off into the desert in search of visions or insights or whatever did not sound romantic at all to me, no matter what photographs, books, or movies might suggest. Even Carlos Castaneda could not complete his training with the shaman. The desert was too much even for him. (Or maybe it was the peyote that became too much.)

But I did plan to wrap myself up in a heavy comforter and join my husband for nighttime sky-gazing before long. Luckily for us, our paved patio was on our rig's shady side, which meant it received no sun during the day to warm up the cement. Therefore, I should be safe from rattlesnakes if I stayed on my patio and didn't walk out in the street. A snake sighting, without a doubt, would destroy my sweet desert dreams.

CHAPTER 28

NO PLACE TO HIDE

I'm smart enough to know alcohol is a depressant, I'm insightful enough to recognize a layer of pandemic sadness beneath my surface, and I'm informed enough to understand we're a country of millions of mildly depressed Americans. This coronavirus crisis has taken a toll on just about everyone's mental health.

Although Michael and I have tucked ourselves into a warm, cozy nest of fellow RVers, I sometimes wonder if there's enough alcohol in California to get me through this. I'm ordering cases of Q Light Ginger Beer Mixers from Amazon and buying 1-lb. bags of limes and 1.75-liter jugs of Tito's Vodka from the grocery store. These Moscow Mule ingredients supplement the many bottles of Apothic Red and boxes of Black Box Cabernet Sauvignon I consume. If this pandemic doesn't turn me into an alcoholic, I'm not sure what could.

We glued ourselves to CNN for CDC recommendations for the Thanksgiving Day weekend. We canceled Thanksgiving Day dinner plans with our Riverside friends, instead eating a lonely but delicious dinner while hunkered down in our RV. Just the two of us. We watched footage of crowded airports and large public gatherings, many of the people unmasked and with no social distancing. We'd heard the CDC's recommendations that no one travel and that families not converge for traditional holiday meals. Then we learned that holiday air travel was down by only 10% from 2019, a time before the pandemic. We listened as scientists advised us the uptick in Covid-19 cases from this Thanksgiving frivolity would be evident about three weeks after the holiday weekend. And honestly, every one of these things made me want to drink.

I'm guessing the virus didn't get the memo of what it was supposed to do. Instead, within a week after the holiday, Covid cases reached their highest levels ever and began increasing exponentially by the day. I soothed myself with a glass of Apothic cabernet sauvignon when I heard this news.

"Listen to this," Michael said. One would've thought he'd just scored Super Bowl tickets from the excitement in his voice. "Hospitals in California are running out of beds. The protocol is that when the number of available ICU beds drops down to 15%, the State will close down all nonessential businesses. We're almost to the point of a shutdown."

This news appeared on a Friday. On Saturday, the California Governor ordered all nonessential businesses to shut down at midnight on Sunday.

"We're in serious trouble," Michael said. "I'm not sure anyone is going to get out of this alive."

"Aren't you being a bit dramatic?" I asked. "We're far from stepping over dead bodies on the sidewalk." I wasn't trying to be cold or crass, but I couldn't help but think that once again, my husband was overreacting. Plus, I was weary beyond words of the hourly updates. "Think we could ever go one day, just one friggin' day, without talking about this pandemic?"

"It's going to get a lot worse before it gets better," Michael said.

"Well, good," I said. "I can sit here. We can order groceries online for curbside pickup. I'll cancel my dermatology appointment and let my skin rot with cancer. I'll wear a friggin' mask and stay six feet away from other people. Not a friggin' problem! But for God's sake, can't we talk about something else? Can we go even one hour without talking about this damn pandemic?"

Despite wanting a drink, I stormed out of the rig and walked in big loops around the RV park for an hour. Guess that's what's the scientists mean by Covid fatigue. I met the criteria. I felt bad that I'd taken my anger out on Michael. But that's depression, and that's how it manifests itself. You turn it either inward or outward. I'd turned it out and lambasted my husband.

By the time I reached the three-mile mark on my stomp around the park, my anger had subsided. However, before I did a complete about-face and turned my anger back inward, I needed to do one more thing. I slinked back home, feeling contrite and embarrassed at my hysterical overactivity, and gave my husband a big hug. I couldn't think of another person I'd rather sit out a pandemic with than my husband, and I couldn't think of another place I'd rather be than right here in Desert Hot Springs, California.

I couldn't help thinking of the adage I'd heard as a child: You can run, but you cannot hide. We'd been on the road since February, running from this coronavirus since March when we first registered its presence in San Antonio. We'd chuckled at all the bullets we thought we'd dodged along the way—Mardi Gras, the AT&T Arena and Riverwalk in San Antonio, the eruption of cases in southern Texas just as we were leaving, our cleverness at hiding out in small towns in New Mexico and Colorado at high elevations all summer, and finding an escape with the Xscapers for the winter in the desert in southern California. I felt like we'd been running for months, and I suppose we had, moving every month or so to safer areas with a lower incidence of the virus.

By the time Christmas arrived, Covid-19 cases had skyrocketed everywhere. Travel had been heavy over the holidays, and scientists warned that January would bring the direst, scariest statistics of illness and death to date.

Then, three days after Christmas, The State of California issued the most terrifying advisory yet. "Do not go to a hospital unless you are dying. There are no beds available, and there are no staff people to see you," said newscasters in Riverside County, where we were now hunkered down. "Our hospitals are filled with Covid patients, and medical care is now being rationed."

"Oh my God," Michael said. "They're now releasing folks from the hospital and sending them home to die. How much worse can this get?"

I certainly didn't know, and I didn't want to think about it. I'd become like an ostrich, wanting to bury my head in the sand so I wouldn't see or hear the horror going on around me. My previous diagnosis of skin cancer, which I'd been trying to get treated during the past ten months on the road, suddenly seemed trivial.

Michael and I both had medical issues, some of which could likely prove far more severe and lethal than my little squamous cell carcinomas. We both needed crowns replaced in our mouths, with tooth decay that could become infected at any time and theoretically turn septic. Michael had Type 1 Diabetes, which was a life-threatening medical condition that could go south at any moment. We both had other known issues lurking in our bodies, and who knew what kind of other unknown problems had buried themselves under our skins. A physician hadn't examined either of us in almost a year. Who knew when either one of us might have a medical emergency from something just as life-threatening as Covid? And now we hear there'd be no treatment available in southern California if that happened?

There seemed to be no place to run. The coronavirus was everywhere. There did not seem to be a safe place anywhere anymore. We could try to go to Australia or New Zealand, but those sane countries wouldn't let an American anywhere near their borders. Desert Hot Springs, where we were, no longer seemed safer or less dangerous than any other place would be. We could keep on running, try to find a safer place than southern California, but I knew there was no place in this country where we could hide.

With that realization, I gave Michael yet another big hug and, this time, a sloppy kiss to boot. Then I made myself a big, refreshing, and soothing Moscow Mule. I was pleased to think the limes grew from trees not two hours away from where we now temporarily called home.

What the hell? I thought. If I can survive this scourge, I can deal with any alcohol problems that pop up. I raised my copper mug in a toast—cheers to me.

Maybe I'd found a place to hide, after all.

CHAPTER 29

ROLLING WITH THE RIG

Although I'd like to, I can't blame everything that goes wrong or happens to our RV on the manufacturer or even on the pandemic. While I can sometimes blame mishaps on external conditions, often it's user error, plain and simple.

When we traded our Class C Four Winds for our new Class A ACE, it was our responsibility to transfer all the stuff from the old rig to the new. Blame it on excitement, exhaustion, frustration, or perhaps our scatterbrained psyches, but there were several items we failed to move. The list included an automatic garage door opener, a 6-ft. folding table, the sensor for an indoor/outdoor thermometer, and an extension cord. Those are the items we remember, but I'm sure there were more. The garage door opener wasn't a big deal—there were several other ways of opening the garage door at our house. We had to replace all the other items, leaving us feeling rather silly.

As readers of *The Reluctant RV Wife* often ask, yes, we christened the black tank in our new motorhome during our maiden voyage. The Gulf Islands National Seashore campground did not have sewer hookups, and we used our bathroom. As we left the park after four nights, we stopped at the dump station to drain tanks.

"I want to do it," I'd said to Michael. "I need to know how to do every bit of work in this thing."

"Be my guest."

My husband is not always this accommodating, and in retrospect, I wish he hadn't been this time either. The drain's angle was awkward, and I inadvertently connected only two of the three notches of the sewer hose to the tank drain opening. When I pulled the lever to open the black tank, the pressure popped the hose off the drain, and contents from the tank gushed onto the asphalt.

"Jesus Christ," Michael yelled. He stepped back, way back, and observed my actions in what looked like horror.

"Oh, stop it, Michael. It's just used food." I'd seen the mistake and closed the lever just as my husband uttered his ungodly shriek. "I've got this," I said, struggling to stay calm. Inwardly I cringed at my stupidity. While the results of my error were not pretty, they were thankfully nothing like the dump station drain fiasco in the Robin Williams RV movie *RV*.

Down the road, months later, we'd have another dumping mishap when our older sewer hose cracked open and leaked. This time, the waste seeped into the ground at our site, but it was only liquid. We learned a hot sun could destroy plastic sewer hoses within months. Since then, we've always stowed an extra hose, just in case an old one springs a leak.

"Hey, Michael, why are these people blowing their horns and pointing at the side of our rig?" We were zipping down Interstate 35 in Texas, leaving San Antonio and heading toward the Rio Grande Valley.

"Don't know. Can't be a flat tire. It's handling okay. I'll pull over the next chance I get and see if anything's wrong."

We found a rest area thirty minutes down the highway. When we looked, we found a basement door swinging in the breeze. "Jeez, all that stuff could have fallen out," I said.

"Doesn't look like it did, though. At least this wasn't a basement we'd crammed too full."

Three months later, this same basement door flew open again when we hit a bump pulling up a steep road to get to our site in an RV park in Green Mountain Falls, Colorado. Something did fall out this time.

On our fourth or fifth day in the park, I happened to talk to a neighbor and mention I was a writer. When I gave her a bookmark with my book's cover, she gasped. "I've seen this cover before! Wait right here."

She scurried to her RV and returned a couple of minutes later with my 18 x 24-in. cardboard poster of the cover of *The Reluctant RV Wife*. When I had bought it over a year ago, Staples had wrapped the poster inside a heavy-duty cardboard case.

"Look," my new neighbor, now a friend, said. "There are tread marks on the cardboard, but the poster isn't damaged. I found it a few days ago when I was walking my dog. I was planning to take it down to the office, figured someone might be looking for it."

"What a serendipity," I said. "I can't even believe this happened. Thank you so much."

A couple of hours later, I signed a copy of my book and walked it down to her. "To say thanks," I said. She and I became Facebook friends, and she made posts promoting my book. I'm still amazed at the incredible fortune that a kind neighbor in an RV park had found a poster on the ground I'd not even realized I'd lost and had returned it to me.

In the RV park in Terlingua, Texas, we found ourselves in a narrow, unlevel, back-in site. I'd become relatively competent at giving Michael hand signals and getting us into tight squeezes without embarrassing myself too much. This time was no exception. However, I'd failed to notice the height of our electric pole. Generally, poles are low enough not to interfere with an extended slide but not this time. When I'd almost fully extended our largest slide, I heard a crunch from the outside. The slide had hit the electric pole. While the mishap didn't damage the pole or disrupt our power, I was heartbroken to have been responsible for the first ding on our new motorhome.

Our failure to retract our step before taking off has been our most expensive and damaging mistake so far. When parked and retracted, this step is about 8-in. off the ground and extends out perhaps 12-in. from the RV side. While we could not extend the step with the engine running, we learned the hard way that we could cold-start the engine and drive away with the step sticking out. As we packed up to leave our campground in the Rio Grande Valley, we forgot to pull the step in.

It seemed like highway construction was going on everywhere in south Texas, with narrow roads, no shoulders, lane shifts, and lots of orange barrels and cones. Our ACE, still new to us, was wider than our Four Winds had been. We'd both flinch when we'd see a large tractor-trailer rig barreling down the road towards us.

Michael drove as we left the RV park. He was building up speed on an under-construction county road when a dump truck approached from the other direction. Michael instinctively eased to the right to give more space to the large truck and possibly save the protruding side mirror on the driver's side.

Bam! At first, we didn't know what had happened, only that an orange barrel went flying off on the right into a ditch. We recognized our error as soon as we pulled over and saw our gnarled, mangled step, now bent to an almost ninety-degree angle, the one we'd forgotten to retract.

We called a mobile RV service at our next stop. Our mechanic, Cory, was a burly, buffed ex-soldier who assured us he could hammer the steel step frame back into shape and make our step functional and roadworthy. "You're lucky that the motor wasn't damaged," he said. "That would've been the most expensive thing to replace."

Cory pulled a sledge hammer out of his van and removed the step from the rig. He placed the step on our wooden picnic table and started banging. For almost three hours, we suffered through deafening clangs and bangs, interrupted only by Cory's animated verbiage about politics and the pandemic during his breaks. I'm sure all our RV park neighbors delighted in the cessation of the noise when Cory stopped banging to talk. However, we suffered either way, for we did not find Cory's political perspectives or medical understandings in agreement with ours.

The pandemic was escalating, and Michael and I believed the science that masks would curb the coronavirus transmission and help keep us safe. We cringed as Cory came in and out of our rig at will, sans mask and sans invitation.

The sun began to sink and, after about two hours, we began thinking about dinner, hoping that our mobile RV tech would soon finish and be on his way. Michael took a ham steak out of the refrigerator, unwrapped it, and put it on a paper plate on the kitchen counter. It'd be ready to cook on the grill as soon as Cory left. I'd already started roasting Yukon Golds and making a salad.

The next time Cory came inside, his eyes widened when he saw the ham steak. "Good God," he said. "You're not going to eat that garbage from China, are you?"

My jaw dropped when Cory made his next move. He turned towards our garbage can, reached in, and pulled out the plastic wrapper in which our ham steak had been packaged. "See that," he said. "Smithfield, a Communist company if ever I've seen one. Didn't you know they import all their meat from China? You have no idea what you're really eating."

Michael and I were both speechless. While we'd had some weird RV mechanics along the way, we'd never had one rummage through our garbage and criticize our food choices.

After about three hours, Cory pronounced our RV step fixed. Although not quite as good as new, the step was functional and retracted almost even with the motorhome side. I decided it wasn't too bad having that step slightly askew. Not only would it remind me of Cory, but it'd also hopefully remind me never to make such a careless mistake again.

When we later told this story to RV mechanics, they had examined our step with amazement. They unanimously agreed Cory had done a remarkable job, the best any of them had ever seen.

⌂

One of the most challenging tasks of RV maintenance was filling our propane tank. While our gasoline tank was in the rear of the RV and we could fill it from either side at a gas pump, our propane tank was on the passenger's side. Truck stops usually sold propane and had easy access for filling up. However, we often found ourselves driving to smaller businesses, like Ace Hardware stores or propane gas dealers, to fill up. These smaller businesses often presented challenges in positioning the rig so the attendant could reach the tank with the hose. Sometimes we had to turn the rig around or back up, and sometimes the required turns were very tight for a 33-ft. motorhome.

I'm happy to report that Michael, not me, put two dings in the RV while positioning the rig for propane fill-ups. The first time was in Colorado Springs and involved a large rock that scraped the paint off a foot-long strip of trim on the passenger side. The second time was in Desert Hot Springs when the rig scraped an iron post and left red paint on a basement door, also on the passenger side. Both accidents stemmed from tight ninety-degree turns required for the propane hose to reach our tank.

I said to Michael later, "I think we shouldn't buy propane in towns with 'Springs' in their names. What do you think?"

He rolled his eyes.

I don't think we're at the point yet of declaring our RV mistakes a comedy of errors, but we might be getting close. It's always reassuring to meet other RVers and to get to know them well enough that they'll share their silly mistakes with us.

We've also learned that if we look very, very carefully, we can find little nicks and dings in almost every RV we see. It comes with the territory, and we'll gladly take those mishaps to continue our adventure.

CHAPTER 30

FULFILLMENT FROM AMAZON

The coronavirus pandemic raged, and our freedom to move eroded by the day. By the time we reached our Xscaper California Home Base in early November, we'd imposed restrictions on ourselves to no longer go into stores except for groceries and prescriptions. In mid-December, the California Governor shut down the State. Online ordering and curbside pickup became our new normal.

Michael had been enjoying online shopping for years. By late spring and throughout the summer, we'd been staying in sparsely populated areas, usually for a month at the time. These small towns had small stores, and we couldn't find many of the things we wanted and needed.

Enter Amazon to the rescue. In the early stages of the coronavirus outbreak, I watched in awe and sometimes in horror as my husband ordered items several times a week. Within a few months, he'd amassed enough KN95 masks to last through three pandemics, or so I thought. I had not yet entered the buying fray.

Shopping has never been my thing. I've always hated it and have had to force myself to go into a department store for jeans or a shoe store for sneakers. When we became RVers, I made the philosophical connection between minimalism and RVing. Adding more stuff to our belongings felt anathema to common sense and inconsistent with my philosophy of not taking more than what I needed. I liked to think that both Henry David Thoreau (ala *Walden*) and Marie Kondo (ala *The Life-Changing Magic of Tidying Up: The Japanese Art of Decluttering and Organizing*) would have smiled upon my shopping and spending habits if they had known. I knew my Depression-surviving parents would have approved wholeheartedly with not wasting money on anything not essential and functional. I'd grown up watching them reuse and recycle everything imaginable, including aluminum foil and plastic bags.

I'd long viewed my husband as a spender, especially with the advent of Amazon and online shopping. In my view, Michael denied himself nothing that might bring joy. (It's a good thing he never invited Marie Kondo in for a consultation. Joy was her standard by which to keep or discard items in one's possession.) My husband had a particular penchant for kitchen gadgets, and I couldn't believe the number of new toys he added monthly to his collection. Now that we lived full-time in an RV, all these gadgets filled a huge drawer in our tiny kitchen. Sometimes I'd pick up a new one I'd not noticed before and ask, "What the hell does this one do?" The answer would usually be something I'd successfully and efficiently done with a paring knife or spoon for decades. I'd heard other women talk of their husbands' love of kitchen tools and the inordinate number of silly, unnecessary ones that jammed their kitchen drawers and cluttered their cupboard shelves. I'd learned to shrug and let it go.

Michael's pleasure shopping extended beyond the kitchen and into electronics, automobile accessories, doodads for his office, workout equipment, and more. When we still owned our house in Tampa, carriers delivered boxes and packages to our front door several times a week. "You've been fulfilled again," I'd say as I dropped the latest arrivals on the kitchen counter. "Come open them up. Let's see what you ordered this time."

Not for me, I'd think. I'll never become such an addicted consumer of goods.

It snuck up surreptitiously, this Amazon ordering obsession. I'm still trying to figure out what drove me to such rampant, out-of-control spending. The shallow explanation undoubtedly related to the pandemic and that I was unconsciously trying to fill the void created by all the losses, limitations, and restrictions in my life. When one feels the bucket emptying, there's a need to plug the holes to stop the drain.

It made me angry, almost sick, that Amazon proved the easiest and most convenient way of trying to refill my bucket. I had no desire to add to Jeff Bezos's coffers. This 56-year-old founder of Amazon was already a multi-billionaire and the wealthiest man in the world. I believed in shopping locally and supporting small businesses owned by families, not giant corporations like Amazon.

Meanwhile, I fell in love with the selection, efficiency, and joy all my Amazon purchases gave at the time of their arrival. I'd ceremoniously unwrap each package, sort of like the unveiling of a precious stone or a Master's painting. It almost didn't matter that my bucket would start leaking the next day again, triggering yet more worthless, useless purchases.

Except for eBooks for my Kindle, I'd never ordered anything from Amazon until 2019. To handle this new buying insanity, I went to Amazon and reviewed my purchasing history. During 2019, I made a total of twelve purchases, a number barely in the double-digits. This number surprised me since I generally wanted to see and touch items before buying. I didn't bother pulling up the itemized 2019 list. I assumed I purchased things I couldn't find in retail stores.

Before leaving Tampa in the RV in mid-February, I'd bought and packed everything I needed for our two-month trip. Even when we kept delaying the trip home, I made do without buying more stuff. As summer approached and I needed cooler clothes, my next-door neighbor, who was emptying our house, mailed the things I wanted to our RV parks. With a summer lull in Covid-19 cases, I risked quick trips into stores several times until mid-October.

Scientists began their dire predictions of what would happen in the fall when temperatures dropped and forced people inside buildings.

They recommended that families forego traditional holiday celebrations and stay home rather than traveling for large family gatherings. My fear escalated, and I vowed to cut out my silly, unnecessary shopping trips for unimportant items.

"Was that necessary?" Michael asked. I'd just gotten home after an aborted trip trying to find tablecloths.

"I wanted a couple of fall tablecloths to put outside. I went to Bed Bath & Beyond, JoAnn's Fabrics, and Walmart. Nada." It was mid-October, and I'd noticed earlier that a neighbor in our park had put burnt orange plastic tablecloths on her two outside tables. "Oh, look, Michael," I'd said. "They're so pretty, and she's even got cut flowers on the tables. Those fall colors are just beautiful. I want to make our site look holiday-ish like that."

It felt like years since I'd done any kind of decorating. Certainly not since we'd left Tampa in this RV. I want to create at least one thing somewhere in our little site that would make it seem like a home, the way I used to cut flowers from my yard and create arrangements for the kitchen counter or the dining room table. I wanted domestic beauty in my life in addition to all the natural beauty of mountains, forests, and deserts. I was disappointed not to have found tablecloths. Later I realized how dumb it'd been to risk infection trying to find something as inane as a tablecloth in the middle of a pandemic.

Even in mid-November, I once went to an outdoor Home Depot garden shop because I thought I'd die without a couple of potted plants to sit outside and look pretty. And they did look pretty, they provided color, and they even attracted hummingbirds. I later realized that the beauty of those flowers and the thrill of those hummingbirds did not hold more value than my good health and continuation of life.

November marks the time I may have lost my mind. It came with the rage-filled realization that this pandemic wasn't over and wouldn't end for months. I finally understood it'd be a long time before I could go back home to see my daughter and friends. This pandemic, with all its ensuing politics, lies, and drama, had changed me. I'd lost everything I'd previously depended on for stability, support, and meaning. The emptiness was unbearable.

I went online to Amazon, and I ordered like a deranged psycho. I ordered outdoor solar lights, an LED floor lamp for my RV office, and a hardback book by an author I didn't like and would probably never read. I ordered matching waffle-weave spa robes for Michael and me to wear to and from the campground's hot mineral springs, knowing full well Michael would probably never even put his big toe in the water. (I was wrong with that prediction and managed to talk him into walking up to the springs. Once.) I ordered Teva sandals, knowing they'd most likely hurt my feet. (They didn't, and I ended up loving those shoes.) I ordered two license plate frames for our RV, enjoying the release of not tossing but cramming the two Big C frames into the garbage can. And this was only a partial list from November's online flurry.

I picked up my pace in December. Maybe it came from realizing there'd be no holiday parties, no Christmas dinners with family and friends, nothing but the two of us sitting out in the god-forsaken desert in a cheap-ass RV listening to the wind howl and hoping we wouldn't catch Covid and die.

I ordered Patchouli oil to wear that only Michael and I would ever smell, a 23" tabletop Christmas tree to go on the RV dashboard, and forty deodorizers for our black tank. I ordered a friggin' case of my favorite brand of ginger beer for Moscow Mules, knowing Tito's Vodka was a lot easier to score from grocery stores than the mixer.

I ordered new king-sized pillows for the bed. I invested in a new vitamin supplement, Biotin, to try to improve my skin and nails, not that anyone would ever get close enough to me again to notice any change. I ordered an electric mixer to make Oatmeal Raisin Cookies, comfort food from my childhood and one of Michael's favorites. I ordered two ultrasonic pest repellents to plug in at opposite ends of the rig. I still felt freaked that several weeks earlier, a person in our group had discovered a rodent in her RV. I ordered a half-dozen pairs of brightly-colored briefs, unable to resist the urge to be a tad outrageous at least somewhere, even if Michael was the only one who would know.

I had ordered all these things by the 10th of December, long before the month ended. I wondered if I should tell Michael how out of control I'd become, ask if he could maybe intervene and make me stop. I didn't want to think about whether we'd have room to pack all this stuff when it came time to leave Desert Hot Springs. My new purchases no longer made me feel quite as good.

I vowed to help myself. I was strong. I could end this foolishness. I took a deep breath and resolved to show more self-discipline. After all, Covid vaccines would be available within days, a new President would take office in January, and scientists predicted that by the end of summer or early fall 2021, life would return to some semblance of normalcy.

Then came a zinger. I was someone who'd experienced anaphylaxis and a complete cardiovascular collapse from an allergic reaction. I might never be a candidate for a vaccine, certainly not ones from Pfizer and Moderna. My immune system had reacted negatively to a foreign sub-stance in the past, and scientists predicted it might happen again in the future. A second infuriating CDC update was when they put Type 2 diabetics above Type 1 diabetics on the list for vaccines. They reasoned that there were so many more Type 2's than there were Type 1's. It didn't seem to matter that the Type 1's were significantly more likely to die than the Type 2's if they contracted Covid-19. And I'm certain they didn't care that my husband was a Type 1. The CDC's prioritization could make me a widow.

Maybe it didn't matter. I was so traumatized and damaged from the past ten months I couldn't imagine my life ever returning to normal. I didn't think I'd ever look at others as anything but death-bearing carriers of Covid. I couldn't imagine brushing against someone in the grocery store without becoming completely unglued. I couldn't imagine ever trusting another politician.

Any belief that the world was a kind, gentle place and that people were innately good and well-intentioned had vacated my psyche, and I didn't think I would ever again be able to find that kind of trust. I felt helpless. Lost.

Then I remembered Amazon and the list I'd already started of new things I wanted to order. If I had a blender, I could make nutritious smoothies for breakfast. My hiking boots were looking a little ratty. Maybe I could order a new pair. *Time Magazine* had just released its 2020 book of photographs that captured the year in review. I'd love to have that book. I hadn't yet bought anything for my daughter for Christmas. Really, I could buy presents for everyone I knew.

I knew how to assuage my helpless and lost feelings. I needed to fill my leaky bucket a bit more. I dug in, let my fingers fly across the keyboard, and browsed offerings in the largest shopping mecca in the world. I ordered a loaf pan to try out a recipe for Cranberry Nut Bread, a cooling rack for subsequent batches of cookies, a new drainer for the kitchen counter, and a heating pad that'd hopefully make the new pain between my shoulder blades go away. Those items seemed like enough for my next order, although I still had many things on that future list. Amazon would most definitely help me keep my bucket filled to the brim.

CHAPTER 31

CHANGED BY A CLOTHESLINE

The pandemic droned on. Horror, anger, and frustration replaced any previous excitement over being a full-time RVer. As summer turned into fall and fall into winter, the CDC warned that Covid-19 cases would mushroom as cold weather forced people inside. We worried for our lives every time the CDC issued new, more restrictive recommendations. Recommendations turned to government mandates following Thanksgiving. I thought I saw D-Day approaching.

Life shrunk. The world took on a dystopian quality. One day bled into the next, indistinguishable and nonmemorable. It was unfathomable that this could be the future of the world, that we might spend the rest of our lives in such a diasporic fog. While this plague had not exiled me from my homeland in sunny Florida—we'd decided to go full time before the pandemic erupted—it had nevertheless wrenched from me my routines, my freedom of movement, my right to live as I pleased. Florida now felt like one of the most dangerous choices of all the states where we could hang out. Before it ended, this pandemic might even claim my life.

I looked around at our socially-distanced campground, and I wondered how all our neighbors whittled away the time. December days in the Coachella Valley were coolish (highs in the low seventies) and windy (winds at 15–18 mph with gusts up to 25–30 mph). At night, temperatures dropped into the upper forties or low fifties. Most days were sunny, with a haze in the distance. We never figured out whether the haze came from low-hanging clouds, sandstorms, or something else. The weather was not conducive for sitting outside unless one loved the wind, which I did not, or had an orientation so the rig served as a windbreaker, which ours did not.

Walking pets seemed to be the most popular outside pastime in the park. Michael and I were among the handful in our group who did not have pets, but these pets and their humans entertained us as they walked by our rig. Some folks seemed never to leave the inside of their rigs except to walk their dogs. As an indication of our lack of outside stimulation during this stay-at-home order from the State of California, I'd even learned to identify some of the dogs by their barks.

Our group included a couple of cat owners. One of our neighbors let her cat outside, and the cat usually stayed close to home. The other cat owner had two cats and walked them on harnesses outside, one cat at a time. I marveled at these two cats, who walked more like leashed dogs than felines.

I chuckled to realize these Xscapers were not the kind to dress their pets up in frilly dresses or mock tuxedos or to place antlers or Santa Claus hats on their heads at Christmas. These dogs, while pampered, mirrored the ruggedness and confidence of their owners. It felt good to have strong, resilient RVers surrounding me. I had no doubt these neighbors would survive this pandemic as well as any other adversity or challenge tossed their way. I resolved to pay more attention and learn from their attitudes.

Michael and I usually logged a few miles several times a week by walking in loops around the campground. An endless and pointless passing of time, but at least we got fresh air and sunshine, we'd tell ourselves. Sometimes we'd walk a mile or so down a lightly-trafficked paved road beside the campground, then turn around and walk back. While easy walking, we found it incredibly boring. Only a rattlesnake sighting might have turned it into something memorable. But then, folks had assured me that this was hibernation season for rattlesnakes and that I didn't have to worry about seeing one in December.

Most of our neighbors seemed to leave the compound a couple of times a week, which was our typical schedule, too. An exception was our perky next-door neighbor, Liza, who went out early almost every morning. She reported catching all the senior shopping times and found stores almost empty of customers. Michael thought Liza took incredible risks in terms of staying safe from Covid-19. I tried to convince him that Liza was just as smart as we were and that everyone took risks, including us. I pointed out that my dear husband took similar risks, like going into a grocery store just to pick up a pint of ice cream and a bag of fresh green beans.

We did not find mornings especially difficult to fill. I usually spent four or five hours at my computer. I had a routine of beginning each day around 6:00 A.M. I'd answer emails, read the *New York Times* daily news briefing and complete its Mini Crossword Puzzle, and then scan *The Tampa Bay Times* and complete its daily Sudoku. These things took an hour or so. I'd then shift to writing for several hours.

Michael spent his morning hours sleeping until 8:30 A.M., then gluing himself to his iPad to read *The Washington Post* and *The Tampa Bay Times*. Next, he'd put on his headphones and listen to CNN, perhaps fiddling around on Facebook towards the end of the morning.

In the afternoons, we'd take walks, sometimes something long enough and strenuous enough to call a wike. Once the temperatures dropped in December, we returned to those desert hiking trails, this time finding them enchanting and enjoyable.

Oftentimes we'd settle down to board games for a couple of hours after our walks. We'd started off our road trip in mid-February with Mexican Train and Rummikub. As the pandemic escalated and our time in the RV increased, we grew bored and tired of these two games. I asked for recommendations on Facebook and received names of about a dozen games, most of which were unfamiliar to me. Gradually, we began adding them to our collection, ordering a new game from Amazon every couple of months. So far, we've added Ticket to Ride—North America, Ticket to Ride—Europe, Azul, Splendor, Stone Age, Blokus, and Pandemic. (Neither of us play traditional card games and, for some reason, have no desire to learn.) At the moment, Blokus is our absolute favorite.

After a couple of hours of games, we'd both read for a while, or if it were 5:00 P.M., Michael would begin watching the news, and I'd continue reading until it was time to start dinner.

We developed a routine of watching a Netflix episode during dinner each night. We went through "Wild Country," "Mad Men," "Waco," "Manhunt: Unabomber," "Shameless," "The Queen's Gambit," "The Tiger King," "The Crown," "Manhunt: Deadly Games," and several others. Currently, we're midway through "Yellowstone," with me wondering how many more episodes I can sit through. As it turned out, I finally convinced Michael to switch to something less violent, and we switched to movies for a while. We found TV watching an effective way of passing the time in the evenings when our eyes were too tired to read and our minds too overloaded to sleep. Such was our boring, isolated daily existence.

In December, when Covid-19 cases spiked and the Governor issued a state-wide lockdown, we shifted away from online grocery shopping with curbside pickup and opted for Instacart. Now we didn't even get to take the car ride into town, leaving us bereft of almost any semblance of our previous lives.

"Well, at least folks aren't dying on the sidewalks," Michael said.

"It might happen. If this keeps up, we could become like Calcutta where they toss dead bodies in the Ganges, just let them float away."

"Not much water out here in the desert," Michael said.

The pandemic made me irritable, judgmental, and restless, and I believed it was doing the same to Michael. Maybe we were a sociable species, after all, Anthony Storr and *Solitude* notwithstanding. I again questioned whether I'd ever recover from this damage to my psyche.

It's strange to look forward to a mundane chore like laundry. But if life becomes small enough, even a walk up to the park's laundry room can break the monotony. Sometimes I searched for items to throw in a pile to wash which didn't even look dirty, like sweatshirts and jackets.

An outside company leased and managed our campground laundry room. A neighbor had warned us the park office absolved itself of any responsibility for handling complaints and problems. Every machine operated with credit or debit cards. Initially, it seemed like a good idea, that never again would we have to scrounge to find quarters to complete a load of laundry.

Just as our neighbor had warned, I soon realized the machines, especially the dryers, had problems. I'd just washed a couple of loads of laundry and had tried almost every dryer in the building. I couldn't find a single one that worked. I stormed to the office to complain.

"I've got two loads of wet laundry, and I can't get a dryer to work," I said, keeping my voice as calm as possible.

"That sometimes happens when it's windy," the employee said. "Everything's done electronically, and I think the wind affects the internet service."

Huh? I thought. I hadn't been having any trouble with internet access on my laptop. "Well, is there any way you can help me? What am I supposed to do with all these wet clothes?"

The staff person shrugged. "I don't know what to tell you. Our owner contracts with this private laundry service to service the washers and dryers. We don't have anything to do with them. Why don't you try calling the company? The number is posted on the wall down there."

I stormed back to the laundry room, where I spent another fifteen minutes trying to get through a voicemail maze with the company and speak with a human, only to finally have the computer voice tell me I had to go online to request service. In frustration, I googled 'laundromat near me' and drove eight miles into town to use dryers in a public laundromat. The place was tight and stuffy, and almost shoulder to shoulder with people doing their laundry. I felt confident I had breathed in coronavirus particles and would die from drying my two loads of clothes. I vowed never to go inside a public laundromat again.

My next-door neighbor, Liza, strung up a short clothesline between her rig and a trailer. Gradually, other makeshift clotheslines popped up in the back-forty where we Xscapers lived. My laundry piled up for a week before I finally found an old-fashioned rope clothesline and wooden clothespins in a Home Depot.

When Liza saw me stringing my line between the fence and the ladder on the back of the RV, she raced out. "Let's string it from your ladder to my ladder. We'll have a long clothesline we can share."

"Great idea," I said. And that's what we did. The Xscapers had left an empty site between each rig, so our clothesline extended about forty-five feet. Although the line sagged a bit when we hung too many heavy, wet items at one time, it nevertheless served its purpose. We never discussed it, but I think we tried to alternate the days we'd do laundry. It felt good, our little communal clothesline. I also found it satisfying organically to hang wet clothes on a clothesline with old-fashioned wooden clothespins.

"I feel like my mother," I'd said to Michael. "This brings back so many memories of growing up on the farm."

Occasionally Liza and I would end up doing laundry on the same day. Something felt almost intimate about hanging shirts, pants, and socks in tandem, each of us beginning at opposite ends of the line, chatting across the vacant site as we each moved closer toward the middle. Maybe it was this conversation at the clothesline that led us to become friends and triggered my saying to her one morning as we each hung up clothes, "This isolation is really wearing me down. Would you two be interested in us maybe sitting in this vacant site some afternoon and just talking for forty-five minutes or an hour? I feel like I'm starved for social interaction."

"Great idea," Liza said. "How about today around two?"

She and her husband, Chris, and Michael and I, converged at the agreed-upon time. We talked for almost two hours. It was a sunny day, temps in the upper sixties, but hardly any wind. Perfect weather. Michael and Chris drank beer, Liza white wine, and I a beloved Moscow Mule. Later that afternoon, I ran into Liza as I returned from the office and she walked her dog.

"That was really great this afternoon," she said. "We should plan to do that at least once a week."

The Santa Ana winds came with a vengeance the next day. We couldn't have sat outside if we'd wanted. I glanced out the window at one point and saw a bobbing lawn ornament tumbling down the street, carried along by the wind. It belonged to neighbors at the end of our row. I rushed out, grabbed the ornament, and returned it to the owners. Later that day, while we were in the front office retrieving yet another Amazon package, a staff person asked if I'd stop by the Andersons' rig and let them know they had several large packages ready for pickup. I did.

The package Michael and I had just picked up contained a portable electric mixer from Amazon. "I'm so excited," I'd said to Michael. "Tomorrow, I'm going to make Oatmeal Raisin Cookies."

"Great," my husband said.

Oatmeal Raisin were his favorites, and I'd had these cookies on my mind for about a week, ever since our online grocery shopper gave us a 2-lb. rather than a 1-lb. box of Quaker Oatmeal.

I made cookies, baking them in our small toaster oven. The small pan held only nine cookies on its single tray. My oven back home in Tampa had been large enough to hold two baking sheets, each sheet containing a dozen cookies. I had to adjust both the oven temperature (from 350 degrees to 375 degrees) and the time (from 8-10 minutes to 11 minutes). No problem. The cookies turned out great. I packed up two bags of still-warm cookies. Michael delivered one bag to Liza and Chris, the other to an elderly couple with health issues on the other side of our rig.

The next day, I experienced an epiphany. Here in the desert, at the peak of this horrific pandemic, ten months and 2,500 miles from home, we'd come full circle. We were now living in the kind of community we'd first heard about at the Spirit of the Road Rally in mid-February in Live Oak, Florida. We'd found a tribe, a band of RVers to call friends. We'd found what RVillage had promised us we'd find: community on the road.

I could only shake my head in wonder.

"Who could ever have predicted what a clothesline would trigger?" I asked Michael.

"What in the world are you talking about? Have you lost your mind?" My husband looked at me as if I'd gone crazy.

"Nope," I said with a smile. "I've found it."

It no longer mattered that we wouldn't get back to Tampa anytime soon or that we had to wear masks, stay out of buildings, and keep six feet away from other people. It didn't even matter that it'd been seven months since we last ate in a restaurant, a month since we'd done our own grocery shopping, almost a year since I'd hugged my daughter.

We were healthy, alive, and free to travel wherever we wanted. The road was our home, and we'd found a community of kindred nomadic souls. I had every expectation that we'd eventually receive Covid vaccines and that we'd live through this pandemic. We were too strong and too smart to give up at this point.

More importantly, if we had found community here with the Xscapers in Desert Hot Springs, we'd find it again. I believed we'd find it wherever we went. Life was good.

I couldn't believe a clothesline triggered such a transformation.

CHAPTER 32

WILL SANTA FIND US IN THE DESERT?

What could anyone say about a Christmas when so many people were hurting and suffering? There was nothing I could add that hadn't already been said many times over and said much more eloquently than I could ever articulate. I almost felt a survivor's guilt that, at least so far, I'd avoided most of the loss and devastation so many hundreds of thousands of people around the world were experiencing. Michael and I were healthy, happy, and relatively safe as Christmas neared. While I complained about what I considered an alienation from others, we were not socially isolated. On the contrary, we'd found community.

"I'm almost afraid to get in the car," I said. "If we got in an accident, we'd never get medical care."

"Yes, you would, Little Cherrie. They've set up emergency medical tents in the parking lot at the Desert Regional Medical Center in Palm Springs. You could have your life-saving surgery outside in the parking lot."

"I don't think that's very funny."

"Of course, it's not. Just be careful not to get in an accident." Michael chuckled. "And you probably want to set the cruise control."

I still bristled every time I thought of that patrolman pulling me over for speeding. I hadn't said anything else to Michael about it, but he must have known it still bothered me.

My ideas about California had previously been of streetcars, hills, and restaurants in San Francisco and big Redwood trees further north. We'd been to San Diego a couple of times, and I loved it, but somehow, I didn't have indelible memories printed in my mind as I did of San Francisco and the Redwoods. This desert would be my third strong California memory.

We were driving out of the RV park, heading for the nature preserve for a long desert hike. Now that temperatures had finally gotten more hospitable for hiking in full sun, I'd come to love the stark loneliness of the parched, rocky ground. Either staff or volunteers had marked the edges of trails with rocks. I could not imagine the number of hours invested in lining miles and miles of paths in an area characterized by so much sameness. Without the stones marking the trails, it'd be easy to become hopelessly lost and wander in circles for hours.

I'd grown to appreciate the almost unchanging environment. It facilitated a turning inward of one's thoughts. While my mood continued to be positive and optimistic, Michael and I were on the same page, thinking it might be time for us to move on.

"Three new rigs pulled into our section of the park today," I said. It was a couple of weeks before Christmas. "When I went up to the office to check for mail, there was a line of rigs waiting to check in up front. This place is going to be bulging at the seams by Christmas Day."

"Let's just hope the Xscapers back here behave themselves," Michael said.

"Looks like the newbies in our group are on the youngish side, like maybe in their thirties and forties. Us old folks are getting outnumbered in this group."

"That's okay. We need just to hunker down and stay to ourselves if we want to stay safe," my rational husband said.

"Do you ever think you might be over-reacting?"

"Nope. The worst is yet to come. This is not the time to start getting sloppy."

I knew Michael was right.

Four days later, I saw a new post from one of the recent arrivals on the Xscapers' private Facebook page. "Oh, my God! Michael, listen to this. This guy asked if anyone wanted to join him in the hot tub tonight at 7:30, and four people said 'yes.' People in the pools or spas don't wear masks in this place. We're doomed."

Michael walked over to read the new post over my shoulder. "You're right," he said. "These younger people don't take this pandemic as seriously as we do."

Our two cohost families had vowed from the onset that this Winter Home Base of Xscapers would make an impact on the community during the holiday season. Before Thanksgiving, they'd spearheaded a food drive, with our donations dropped off at a food bank in nearby Cathedral City, California. Our hosts' philanthropic urges went into overdrive as Christmas approached.

"We've found this group home right across the street for abused and neglected boys," one of the leaders said. "We're going to look into our group buying Christmas toys for those children this year. It'd be a great thing for us to do."

Curiosity got the best of me. During one of our afternoon walks, I suggested to Michael that we walk down the secondary road near the park and check out the group home. Management had posted the name of the facility in front of the main building. When we got back to the rig, I googled the name to see what I could find out.

"It's a religious thing," I said to Michael. "Very mixed reviews here on the internet. A couple of people wrote the place is so bad it should be shut down."

"What does that mean? Think you ought to say something to our hosts?"

"Let me think about it for a couple of days. I'd feel a lot better if our donations went to a place like the Salvation Army. They've been around forever, and they know all the reputable and worthy programs in the community. I'd trust them to decide who gets what. If this group home over here is legitimate, it'll be on the Salvation Army's list."

I thought about our group's desire to give to the community during the holiday season. Our hosts had sounded thrilled at finding a group home nearby where the contributions would feel so personal. The boys from the group home rode bicycles through our park, and we'd all seen the boys. I decided to bite my tongue and not express my social work misgivings to the hosts. I felt sure those boys fit the criteria of neediness, and the world needed all the goodwill and generosity it could muster these days. It was none of my business whether this group home was legitimate or whether established agencies in the community had vetted the services it provided. Perhaps none of it mattered anyway.

The charitable instincts among the Xscapers escalated daily. The leaders talked with the management of the group home and decided to raise money to buy bicycles. The facility housed twenty-four school-aged boys, and most of their bicycles were broken and beyond repair. Through Facebook calls for donations, every Xscaper rig chipped in between $50 and $75, including ours.

Our hosts spent several days combing Walmart stores and other outlets, searching for both bicycles and other toys. On the Sunday before Christmas, they scheduled a campground gathering for bicycle assembly and gift wrapping. They'd bought six bikes, which was all they could find in stock in nearby stores. With leftover money, they purchased individual gifts for every boy living in the group home and other toys the boys could share.

"What are we going to do about all of this?" I asked Michael on the Saturday before the planned gift-wrapping party.

"I think these people are all going to get Covid," my surly husband said. "But they're not going to give it to me. I'll have no part of a group party where people are working that close together wrapping presents and putting bicycles together."

"It's outside," I pointed out. "And I'm sure they'll all wear masks."

"Doesn't matter. Have you thought of all the stores those people were in during the past week searching for bicycles? Then later going to buy all those individual gifts? I think we ought to be gone somewhere, like hiking, when this party starts."

"You've certainly got a bah-humbug attitude." I thought about it some more. "What I don't like is that they scheduled this gift-wrapping and bicycle assembly at the time when we were supposed to have our group gift exchange. If we don't go, what'll we do with this stupid gift we bought? I wish they'd kept the two events separate."

"I'll have no problem whatsoever disposing of that Hickory Farms gift basket," Michael said. "It'll be a nice holiday treat for us."

"Well, we can look out the window and see what they're doing when the time comes. Maybe it'll look safe enough to you that we could walk down, be a part of the group."

"You can go if you want. I want no part of it."

Holidays are often, maybe usually, stressful. Back home, Michael and I would invariably be on different pages regarding how to handle family. Sometimes we'd receive conflicting invitations for parties or get-togethers. How much money to spend, how many people to include, what time of the day to have the big meal if we were cooking at home—the potential areas of disagreement seemed never to end.

Thanksgiving had been a non-stressful, happy, relaxed holiday. Why couldn't Christmas have been the same?

I thought I'd detached from my previous lifestyle and the former world rather well. I thought I'd coped better than average with a pandemic that had already sickened friends, killed a couple of acquaintances, and turned my world upside-down. I thought I'd found community with RVers out here in the desert of southern California. I thought cash contributions to charities of my choice were plenty sufficient to help spread holiday cheer. I thought that after almost eleven months of nonstop togetherness, my husband and I would finally have reached enough of an understanding to at least be able to talk things through and compromise when we saw situations from our different perspectives.

🛻

Guess you'll get your way again, I thought, and hated myself for feeling resentful. Our Xscapers group had begun gathering down at the usual meeting spot in the campground. I watched the hosts set up tables and bring out huge boxes of toys for the group to wrap. The guys had set up several other tables, quite a distance apart, and I assumed they'd use them for assembling bicycles.

We wouldn't be a part of the group, however. We were slinking off in the car to go to the Big Morongo Canyon Preserve, about thirty minutes to the north of the RV park. I hated that we'd failed to leave the park before the group started arriving. I felt embarrassed, maybe even like a traitor, that we were so blatantly shunning the group's effort to bring joy to the lives of twenty-four boys, all of whom had been born at the wrong time in the wrong place and to the wrong set of parents. But then, social workers had learned decades ago that the world was not always a fair and just place.

Two hours later, when we returned home from our outing in the most beautiful and glorious canyon we'd found so far in the Desert Hot Springs area, our group was finishing up its gift exchange. Michael and I dragged our lawn chairs down and sat near the rear of the group. Our unopened Hickory Farms gift basket sat on the sofa in our rig.

The juxtapositions and absurdities of our choices overwhelmed me, and I crumbled emotionally at the toll this pandemic had taken on us all. In so many ways, it had turned every one of us into hypocrites, turned us against each other, and led to a world in which no matter what decisions we made, we'd be both applauded and criticized, viewed as both right and wrong.

Michael was right—these Xscapers were taking risks working so closely together in their efforts to bring holiday cheer into the lives of others. At the same time, the Xscapers were right—the most magical, emotional time of the year was upon us, and maybe it was okay to sacrifice personal safety to bring happiness to others. Perhaps it would have been okay to lower our guard for just one day for the greater good of the world. I almost believed it would have been justifiable.

The Escapees RV Club issues a weekly *Escapees Member News*. On Tuesday, December 22nd the newsletter appeared in my email. The newsletter included a featured group photograph of the Xscapers California Home Base group with six bicycles and a massive pile of wrapped presents. The headline read, "Escapees Give Back!" The article reported that our group raised over $2000 for bicycles, helmets, toys, toiletries, and individual gifts for the twenty-four residents of a local group home for neglected and abused boys.

I studied that photograph in the *Escapees Member News* very carefully, pleased to note that Michael and I had not been the only group members who failed to participate. I also noted that most of the RVers stood shoulder-to-shoulder in the photograph, far closer together than the CDC recommendation of six feet. When I mentioned my observation to Liza a few days later, she said, "We were that close together only for the few seconds it'd taken for them to take the picture." I could only sigh. What else could I do?

I'd found the answer to my original question, though. Yes, Santa had found us out here in the desert. I almost wish he hadn't.

CHAPTER 33

'TIS THE SEASON

Christmas neared, and my sense of isolation and loneliness increased exponentially. Thanksgiving had been okay, but Christmas without any friends and family felt unbearably bleak. The influx of new people into the Xscaper group turned the volume up on our fears of catching Covid but somehow did nothing to improve our common sense.

When Michael and I made our four-month reservations to hunker down with the Xscapers in southern California, we didn't expect to see so many RVers coming and going from the group. While the shortest amount of time anyone stayed was a month, others stayed six weeks, two months, three months, and the entire four months of the reserved time. As Xscapers moved on, other Xscapers came in to take their places. At any given time, the back-forty section of the RV park, where the Xscapers stayed, housed about twenty rigs. Slightly over half of the rigs had couples, two of the couples had either one or two children, and the other rigs contained solo travelers, most often women.

November with the Xscapers had spoiled us. Most of the RVers at the west end of the park, opposite our end, were solo RVers, and they infused excitement and energy into the group. They're the ones who'd invite everyone down for the sunset happy hours, who'd arranged to eat Thanksgiving dinner together as a group, and who threw themselves a goodbye party with grilled salmon for everybody at the end of November before they left.

The new December arrivals tended to be couples, not solo travelers, and they tended to be a bit older and less gregarious. Was it because of age, or because couples weren't as needy of social interaction as single travelers, or was it fear because Covid-19 infections had escalated following the Thanksgiving holidays? We decided it was probably a combination of all the above.

By Christmas week, Michael and I had become almost paranoid. On the Monday before Christmas, we freaked when our Albertsons grocery store canceled our online order. The store sent a text that it was due to high demand. We ended up rushing into Albertsons and grabbing whatever we could remember that'd been on our list. It was the first time we'd been inside a grocery store in a month, and I felt like my heart would burst out of my chest with anxiety.

"Oh, my God." I let out a gasp. We were in the car, driving back to the RV park with our grabbed grocery items stuffed in the back of the car. "Do you realize this is Monday? Christmas is Friday, and we don't have a dinner planned. The least we can do is have a nice dinner at home, don't you think?"

Michael agreed and volunteered to scout out butcher shops the next day and score us a standing rib roast to cook in our Weber Q-Grill. Or if not a roast, at least a chicken we could stuff with dressing and pretend it was a turkey.

I went with Michael on his Christmas dinner entree shopping mission. With spending so much time isolated in the motorhome, I welcomed any opportunity to see something different than our current views out the RV windows. We spent two hours, drove over thirty miles, and went to four other butcher shops trying to find a standing-rib roast. We had no success. In retrospect, the anxiety I felt with each dash into a meat market and a quick scan of the meats on display probably took at least a year off my life because of the stress.

"Let's just go to Whole Foods," I finally said, exasperated. "I don't care how much it costs. I just know they'll have it, and it'll be Prime A quality."

Michael agreed and googled Whole Foods on his phone. Nine miles and twenty minutes later, we found the store. We also found a line that wrapped around the block of folks waiting to get in. We agreed to keep driving.

"No holiday meal is worth risking our lives," Michael had said.

Later that afternoon, as we sat with Liza and Chris in the sunshine sipping alcoholic beverages at two o'clock in the afternoon, we told our frustrating, disappointing story of failing to find an entree for our holiday meal. (Yes, I sorely needed to reevaluate my drinking behavior.)

"Listen," Liza said. "I'm making a run to Jensen's market in the morning. Why don't you come with me? We'll mask up, keep the windows cracked, and you can find your standing rib roast or whatever while I pick up a few things? It'll be quick and safe."

"What kind of store is this Jensen's?" Michael asked.

"It's an upscale market, probably better than Whole Foods," Liza said. "It's the kind of place you go for holiday shopping, to get really special, high-quality items."

I considered Liza's invitation and hesitated. Just going into Albertsons yesterday to grab a few items had scared the bejesus out of me. Thoughts of that long line of people outside Whole Foods earlier today raced through my mind. If Jensen's was trendier than Whole Foods, their lines might even be longer, plus tomorrow would be a day closer to Christmas, making it even worse.

However, the thought of getting inside a car with someone outside my household was the thing that freaked me out. How long had it been since I'd been that close to another person? The trip would take at least 30 minutes, more than enough time for Covid transmission if either of us were unknowingly positive. I'd just walked into four different butcher shops this morning, and yesterday I'd gone into an Alberton's. And Lord only knows how many stores Liza had walked into during the last few days in a flurry of holiday planning and shopping. Either or both of us might well be positive.

"Let me think about it," I finally said. "What time will you leave in the morning?"

"Oh, early. Around nine or so," Liza said. "Just text or call me with what you decide to do."

I didn't have to think long. As soon as we got back to our rig, I said to Michael, "I think I'm damaged for life. I can't get into a car with someone, not even if we were both wearing three KN-95 masks."

"Let me try again to find a roast or something. Maybe Jensen's has an online or telephone option for ordering, and Liza could pick up the order for us in the morning." When he googled Jensen's, the market came up as Jensen's Finest Foods. I'd been right—Jensen's sounded more upscale, or at least more pretentious, than Whole Foods.

A few minutes later, Michael asked, "How would you like a Filet Mignon, Roasted Asparagus, and a fully-loaded Twice-baked Potato for a nice Christmas Eve dinner? We could pick it up a 5:00 P.M. on Christmas Eve."

"Perfect," I said. "Let's do it."

The next morning, around 8:00 A.M., as I sat tapping away on my laptop, I suddenly heard a howling wind outside. The predicted Santa Anas had arrived to usher in another cold front, this one for Christmas Day. I hopped up to check on our folding chairs and any other items we might have left outside that could blow away.

I noticed that Liza's car was not at their rig. She left early, I thought. I bet she's relieved I said no to her invitation.

As it turned out, Michael and I did not enjoy a Christmas Eve dinner of Filet Mignon and the delicious anticipated sides. As we drove to Jensen's to pick up our special dinner, the low air pressure alert on the car popped up, and we spent forty-five minutes trying to find a tire store or a service station open on Christmas Eve to check our tires. Finally, at two minutes before six, we found a Chevron Station just as the mechanic was closing for the night. He graciously checked all the tires and filled a low one with air. (Thankfully, it did not appear to be a punctured tire with a slow leak.) By the time we'd taken care of the car, night had descended, and we were in unfamiliar territory in total darkness.

No problem, we thought. We'll just google Jensen's, and the GPS will direct us to the store. Unfortunately, Jensen's had three locations. Two of the sites were full specialty markets and the third was more like a convenience store. Michael had written down the address of the store where he'd place the order. Somehow, the slip of paper had gotten lost in the car, and Michael couldn't remember the street name. We took a chance and programmed the GPS for the nearest Jensen's.

We chose badly and ended up at the convenience store. A young employee stood out front smoking a cigarette. We asked her which Jensen's offered the special take-out dinners. She didn't have a clue but assured us she could sell us a wonderful dinner of rotisserie chicken, beans and rice, and fajitas.

By this point, Michael and I were exhausted, famished, and arguing. It didn't take long to agree that we should buy the cafeteria-style meal, which had probably been sitting in warming dishes for hours, and go home.

Our Christmas Eve dinner consisted of cooked-to-death chicken and dry rice and beans. We weren't even sure what the fajitas were for and never touched them. Lots of red wine salvaged the meal for me, but Michael felt disgusted and disappointed by the entire experience.

Not having scored a lovely standing-rib roast and it now being too late for any further shopping, I made meatloaf on Christmas Day. It seemed appropriate. Meatloaf was one of my ultimate comfort foods, and this was a holiday that left me longing for comfort.

I hoped that once Christmas was over, collective self-discipline would reappear in all of us Xscapers, and common sense would win out over our current holiday-related lapses in judgment.

I realized I had many, many things to celebrate this holiday season, perhaps more than I'd ever had in my life. But as I counted my blessings, I felt especially relieved for one small blessing that'd come to our neighbor around the corner and possibly to all of us Xscapers in the park.

"Hey, Andrea," I called out. I was returning to our rig from the office with my daily Amazon delivery. "What's the story with your mouse?"

My neighbor laughed and walked closer to the street to chat. "I caught him two nights ago, and it wasn't a mouse after all. It was a rat!"

My jaw dropped. "How'd you finally get him?"

"With a sticky trap. That damned thing had managed to steal cheese and peanut butter from traps and had eluded sticky traps for several days. Finally, he got a back leg caught on one of the traps in a basement. When I found him, he was still alive but just about dead from struggling."

"Do I dare ask how you dealt with a live rat?"

"I picked him up with my long BBQ tongs and drowned him in a bucket of water. For the first time in about three weeks, Marco (her dog) and I both got a good night's sleep last night. What a relief."

I returned home and immediately gave Michael the update. "There's at least one thing I no longer have to worry about," I said. "It doesn't sound like Andrea's mouse brought in a spouse and start breeding. If he had, every rig back here could have become infested with rodents."

"What in the world are you talking about?"

"You know, this back-forty of the RV park isn't going to turn into a rat's nest. I probably shouldn't tell you, but I've had these visions of rodents procreating and invading other rigs, eventually leading to an infestation and domination of the entire Xscaper area." I paused to catch my breath. "I'm thinking Andrea's mouse, rat, whatever it was might have been sterile. Or maybe just an outcast."

"Nah," Michael said. "It was just an old desert rat, just like some of these Xscapers. I can only imagine what might blow in next."

CHAPTER 34

LET THE WINDS BLOW

"You're not going to want to be here in January and February," Bill, our new RVing friend, said to us over the Thanksgiving holidays. "When those Santa Ana winds blow in, gusts can get up to 100 mph."

"You've got to be kidding," I said. "The Xscapers wouldn't bring us here if it got that bad. That's like a Category 2 hurricane."

"Just the gusts get that high. Sustained winds are probably more like 40 or 50 mph," Bill had said.

Diane jumped in to the conversation. "We used to live in this area, over in the Thousand Palms area. One time I got caught in a sand storm trying to get home. The sand was so thick I couldn't see more than a few yards ahead of me."

"Yeah, and when we looked at the car the next day, that sand had taken off the paint around the front headlights," Bill added.

I sat in silence, stunned. Michael also appeared incredulous.

Craig laughed. He and Arline were also familiar with this area, frequently coming in their fifth wheel for long weekends. "See all those windmills off to the south?" He pointed towards the dozens of mammoth-sized, white three-bladed turbines that generated power. Most of the blades hardly moved on this calm day. "This entire area north of Interstate 10 is a wind tunnel tucked between all these mountain ranges.

Palm Springs, just fifteen miles south of here, doesn't get winds like they do here."

I'd turned to Michael. "Think we need to get out of here at the end of December? I don't want my car destroyed."

"Just stay home when the Santa Anas come," Diane said with a laugh. "You'll be okay. Besides, those sandstorms happen in the desert areas closer to the Interstate, where the sand is so loose. I'm sure you've noticed it. There are more rocks up here, closer to Desert Hot Springs."

The conversation moved to other topics, but the image of 100 mph sand storms stayed with me. It was just another thing for me to fret and stew over. Covid, rattlesnakes, and rats would have been more than enough to keep my anxiety levels high. Now I had to add 100 mph sandstorms that could ruin our car and RV to my list of worries.

Wind speeds picked up in late December. I said to Michael. "I guess this is our warning for what January and February will be like. You still okay with staying here?"

"Sure. I am. You're the one who was freaking out at the sandstorm story. Which, by the way, I think Bill was exaggerating. He liked seeing you get so hysterical."

"Oh, cut it out."

"Are you still thinking we need to leave?" Michael asked.

"Nope. I'm good. I like it here, and I think we need to stay as long as we can."

"What has come over you? Here we are in the middle of the worst pandemic the world has ever seen, political unrest that could lead to the next civil war, hospitals filled with Covid patients." Michael paused to catch his breath. "But anyway, now you're just as calm and relaxed as you can be. What gives?"

"You're the one who's done the about-face. A few days ago, you swore we were all going to die because our fellow Xscapers wrapped a few Christmas presents for some needy kids."

"We just need to keep our guard up, make sure we keep our distance," Michael said.

"I'm having good dreams these days. Two nights ago, I dreamed I was dancing, and last night I dreamed I was going back to school. I think it was Stetson University, and I was going to study interior design. How crazy is that?" It was crazy. I'd gone to Stetson University in Deland, Florida, my freshman year in college, and the school did not have a program in interior design. And even if it had, the subject wouldn't have interested me any more back then than it did today.

"I think all this means something, Michael. Not that I believe in dream interpretation, but I think these dreams mean I've accepted and embraced my new life."

"I think it means you're psycho," my less-than-impressed husband said. "Have you considered it might mean you've lost your mind?"

"Nope. I think it just means that I finally understand what this year has been all about, and I'm now coming out on the other side."

My current happy mood reminded me of peak moments or experiences, a concept originally developed by Abraham Maslow in 1964. Maslow used the term to refer to a blissful, ecstatic feeling that could occur at unexpected and surprising times. Maslow saw it as an altered state of consciousness, often achieved by self-actualized individuals. It was not necessarily about the activity itself but rather about the euphoria that occurred while engaging in the activity.

Not that I would ever be so arrogant as to describe myself as self-actualized, but I'd had an experience like that when I was forty-one years old. It'd been during a wild, lost, mid-life crisis following a divorce. I'd bought a motorcycle and gotten involved with an alcoholic biker. We'd taken off one summer for a trip to the annual motorcycle rally in Sturgis, South Dakota. (My ex-husband assumed parental duties, and my mother pitched in to assist while he worked.)

The boyfriend and I had gotten as far as Omaha, Nebraska, when we had a huge fight. In anger, I took off for Tampa while he continued to

Sturgis. My peak moment occurred as I rode my motorcycle through the Smoky Mountains on my way home. The beauty of the surroundings, the rush of being on a bike, the feeling of being a part of the scenery rather than an observer of it, and the exhilaration of leaving an inappropriate boyfriend to travel across the country by myself produced a euphoria unlike anything I'd ever known. I remembered thinking: if I should go over the side of this mountain right now and die, it would be okay. I am where I need to be and doing what I should be doing.

I'd never since experienced such a feeling of perfection, of empowerment, of happiness like I felt at that moment.

Until now . . .

While it wasn't a sudden 'aha moment' like my motorcycle trip through the mountains had produced, a similar overwhelming feeling of rightness had enveloped me over the clothesline strung between our RV and Liza and Chris's. Here in the middle of the desert, with the Santa Ana winds howling and the emotional holiday season behind us, I knew I was where I needed to be, doing what I needed to be doing.

The year 2020 had been horrifying, terrifying, and disorienting. We'd sacrificed almost every possession we owned when we sold our house over the summer.

We'd become alienated physically and to some extent emotionally from family and friends.

Both Michael and I needed medical and dental care but were unwilling to risk going into doctors' offices to obtain it.

We were several thousand miles from home, in unfamiliar geography, and surrounded by people we didn't know.

We'd spent a lonely Thanksgiving and an even lonelier Christmas.

A week earlier, I'd despaired that I'd never feel happy again, that I'd never again achieve any sense of stability and peace.

Now, I thought those Santa Ana winds maybe blew in more than just sand. Perhaps they blew in some desert Zen and ushered in good dreams, contentment, and the understanding we'd made the right decisions during the past eleven months. Maybe they'd blown in these euphoric feelings of being exactly where I needed to be, doing what I was doing.

I'm sure my husband would find this absurd, but I believe I can also thank those Santa Ana winds for the communal clothesline that triggered all these thoughts a couple of months earlier. After all, had the winds not caused the dryers in the laundry room to malfunction, would Liza and I have ever ended up with a shared clothesline? I think not. The clothesline led to the friendship, which led to the happy hours, which mitigated the acute social isolation and ultimately led to an acceptance and embrace of my current circumstances.

Maybe I didn't want those winds ever to stop. I was happy.

CHAPTER 35

NOW WHAT?

"Idiots," I'd muttered to Michael as we watched the evening news. "I'm so glad Kate hadn't wanted to come out during the holidays." Before we'd left Florida almost a year ago, I'd promised my daughter I'd send her airfare to fly out to visit between Thanksgiving and New Year's. But that was long before the pandemic, and now I'd have been afraid for her to travel.

While the United States led the world in the incidence of Covid-19 cases, I couldn't help but think we also led the world in stupidity. This country knew what it needed to do, but no one dared to take charge and make it happen. How had a public health crisis become so political? What had happened to our humanity, our concern for the well-being and safety of others? That all these Thanksgiving and Christmas travelers would put their desire to spend holidays with their families over human life appalled me.

The surge in Covid-19 cases three weeks after Thanksgiving was worse than scientists had predicted. Travel over the holidays had been down only 10% over previous, non-pandemic years, despite warnings and pleas from scientists to stay home. Michael and I had watched national news with horror and dread during the long Thanksgiving weekend. I admitted to feeling somewhat sanctimonious as we ate our stark little turkey breast dinner all alone in our rig.

"Christmas will be better," I said. "People will have come to their senses by then and will know they have to stay home, don't you think?"

"Yeah, right," my sarcastic husband said. "Want to place any bets?"

Hope arrived in mid-December with the announcement that vaccines were on their way. The pharmaceutical company Pfizer received the first Congressional and CDC approval for its vaccine, with their research showing 95% effectiveness. The country applauded as news channels showed endless video clips of UPS and FedEx trucks pulling out of warehouses and airports to deliver the vaccine to frontline healthcare workers.

Within a week, Moderna, another pharmaceutical company, received emergency approval for its vaccine. Moderna's version was based on the same science of tricking the body into developing its own antibodies to the coronavirus. Hopes soared even higher. At last, anchors on the major networks had encouraging news that brought relief and joy.

Diagnoses of Covid-19 seemed to soar in direct proportion to promises that the pandemic end was in sight. Scientists and some politicians begged the public not to relax, not to let down on the disciplines of wearing masks, socially distancing, and staying home. They warned the pandemic would not subside until a large number of people received the vaccines.

"Our luck this time is horrible," I said to Michael. "While we might be stuck out here in this little isolated desert town, California has the highest number of Covid cases in the country right now."

"I'm well aware of that, but where the hell would you want us to go?"

"Well, maybe somewhere where we could get medical care if you fell and broke your leg?"

"I could probably get a cast slapped on in a makeshift tent somewhere," Michael said with a laugh. "No one's getting medical attention for much of anything anymore. California's not the only state that's run out of hospital beds. There's nowhere to go right now."

"What happened to our luck earlier in the year, when we were getting out of places right before things got bad?" I asked. I remembered New

Orleans, San Antonio, fleeing the Rio Grande Valley just before Hidalgo County became the most infected place in the entire county for a short while. "We were doing so well there for a while."

"There was no consistent national leadership in dealing with this virus. That's what happened, Little Cherrie. The worse has yet to come."

If he doesn't stop calling me that diminutive, ridiculous name, I'm going to scream. I didn't say anything, however. I realized we needed as much lightheartedness as possible, and my husband thought his little nickname for me was charming and endearing. I added it to my small but growing list of items I'd deal with when the pandemic ended if I was still alive.

We already knew several people who had died from Covid-19, and we were up to about a dozen folks we knew who'd had the disease. Most of them still struggled, weeks and months later, trying to regain strength and their previous states of health. A good friend described a 'brain fog' eight months after doctors declared her negative for Covid. Another friend experienced severe gastrointestinal issues during Covid and needed surgery two months after doctors pronounced her negative. Yet another friend experienced heart complications requiring follow-up months after doctors pronounced him a Covid survivor.

"You realize," I said, "that regardless of how careless we may think all our Xscaper neighbors back here might be, we've been here about two months, and not a single person in our group has gotten sick."

"You're right," Michael said. "Maybe when they come and go every day, they're heading out to hike or do something outside rather than going into stores. Or maybe they're going for curbside pickup of stuff."

"I think we've been too harsh and critical. I think this is a very conscientious group and that they take fewer chances because they're in this group. I think they take this community thing seriously."

I'd also come to believe that just like in a real family, not everyone would make decisions identical to mine. My job was to keep my mouth shut, just as I'd learned to do with parents, siblings, children, and extended family.

It dismayed me to learn two days before Christmas, Florida had prioritized giving the vaccine to people over sixty-five. "Crap seven ways to Sunday," I screamed at the irony. "Florida's been the most absurdly out-of-control state in the country, so Covid-ridden we wouldn't have dreamed of going back. Now, I'm so sorry we aren't there. We're never going to get the vaccine out here in the desert of southern California."

"Yes, we will, Little Cherrie. Just calm down. I've been monitoring. We're in group 1-C. That's the third tier, the one for people over sixty-five. We'll probably get the vaccine in mid-January."

"How? We're don't know a single doctor out here. We're not residents. What makes you think we have a ghost of a chance to get vaccinated out here in the friggin' desert of southern California?" I felt tears of frustration welling in my eyes, suddenly furious at everything and everybody.

Should we have been surprised that problems arose with the vaccines' release and distribution, that things did not go as quickly and smoothly as the government had predicted? As 2020 ended, it was apparent that no one at any government level had prepared for an orderly distribution of the vaccines and an efficient injection of the drug into arms. The Warp Speed program that had funded pharmaceutical research and facilitated the government approval of vaccines had predicted that by the end of the year, twenty million Americans would have received vaccinations, beginning with frontline healthcare workers. The year ended with less than three million being vaccinated.

A couple of weeks later, I felt awful when I chuckled about Florida's vaccination fiasco. Mixed in with my short-lived regret at not being in Florida, where I'd erroneously believed I'd receive a vaccination immediately, I felt terrible for all my over-sixty-five friends who had been unable to snag appointments for the shots. I truly wanted them to receive vaccinations.

I hated myself for finding the continued ineptitude of vaccine distribution amusing. This past year had turned me into a sardonic skeptic. I could only hope I'd again see the world with awe and wonder once science, politicians, and the people in this country had defeated this coronavirus.

"How soon do you think you'll get vaccinated?" I asked Kate during a phone call. She was a paramedic with a fire department in Florida. I'd been holding my breath for her safety, knowing she worked on an ambulance transporting Covid-19 patients to emergency rooms. I worried daily about my daughter getting sick.

"Oh, I don't know," she said in response to my question. "We got an email about it a couple of days ago, but I haven't bothered to read it yet."

I bit my tongue to mask my shock. "But aren't you eager to get vaccinated? Don't you worry about catching it?"

"No, not really. We have all the PPE we need, and the truck is sanitized between every transport." She paused as if knowing what she'd say next might not meet with my approval. "I'm not sure I'm even going to get the shot. It's just too new, developed too quickly. I might wait a few months, see what happens down the road."

I felt a surge of relief a couple of weeks later when Kate texted me that she would be vaccinated at work. Two days later, she texted me a photo of the needle in her arm to reassure me. I'll never know whether the fire department mandated its employees receive the vaccine or whether my daughter made her own decision. It no longer mattered. I was just happy to know my daughter was now protected.

Kate's mistrust of the vaccine was not an outlier, however. Reports of people refusing to take the vaccine, even frontline healthcare workers, began to appear. Other groups also spoke out, voicing concerns over the safety of the vaccine. The Black community expressed mistrust, reminding the scientific community of the Tuskegee syphilis studies of infected Black men during the 1930s. Researchers had left infected men untreated from syphilis for research purposes, never informing them of the studies or obtaining consent. Millions of Trump supporters still viewed the pandemic as a hoax, fake news. Religious zealots believed God would protect them, making masks and social distancing unnecessary. Many maintained that deaths from Covid-19 were grossly exaggerated, that Covid was probably no more deadly than the common flu that'd been around for decades, or that doctors falsely reported diagnoses to make more money.

A new mutation of Covid-19 appeared in the United Kingdom, France, the United States, and soon across the world. Researchers described this new variant as more contagious than the current strain. Scientists assured us existing vaccines would be effective against this new strain. I had to wonder, though. What about further mutations in the months ahead? Or what about the next virus that would appear in humans? Those wet markets in China, Africa, and other far-away places still existed.

"We're not going to get the vaccine for months, are we?" I said to Michael. "When do you think it'll be? April or May, maybe?"

"Well, I'd certainly hope it'd be sooner than that, but who knows? There's really nothing we can do but wait." I realized he'd abandoned that earlier prediction that we'd be vaccinated by mid-January.

I knew my husband was right. We had just to sit tight and be patient. Wait, in other words. Some scientists predicted things in the country would have calmed down by the end of February, and others felt certain it'd be the end of next summer or early fall before any semblance of order returned. How could someone like me make sense of a zeitgeist that changed by the hour, of a world that changed by the day?

If thoughts like these weren't grim enough, a couple of days later, the World Health Organization said, "This may not be the big one," suggesting that even more virulent pandemics were likely in the future.

🚐

Two days before Christmas, I sat perched in the passenger seat in my RV office, my laptop ready as I reined in my thoughts. The Santa Ana winds howled as the temperature dropped. Tonight would be our coldest weather yet in Desert Hot Springs—falling to the low forties if weather predictions held. I could see the San Jacinto Mountains out the front windshield. Tomorrow they'd be dusted with snow.

We'd been on the road almost eleven months. We'd left home, friends, and family to test out our new motorhome on a two-month road trip. We'd had every expectation we'd be back home by mid-April.

Instead, we became stranded, unable to travel. Within a few months of the pandemic, we'd come to view our RV as a cocoon, the safest place we could be. We believed it would keep us safe as we ran for our lives from Covid-19. So far, it had.

I've heard, read, and seen enough Covid-19 stories to understand Michael and I could both be dead in two weeks. Or even worse, that one of us could die while the other one lived.

I further understood this pandemic had changed me. Even if Covid-19 faded into nothing but a bad memory, I'd never return to the person I'd been before the pandemic struck.

Out of all the fears and disruptions of the past year, a calm arose from deep inside as I stared off at the mountain peaks. I'd finally come full circle from where I'd been at the beginning of this road trip.

I again felt the excitement that'd characterized our trip at its onset, the awe and wonder of the RVillage Rally, where I'd first heard Bob Wells posit the notion that nomadism was the most natural way to live. It had been so exciting making friends with Jack and Nadyne Huber, David and Denise Ordonio, and Les and Kerry Jones at the rally, and knowing we'd stay in touch.

I thought of Arline and Craig Bringhurst, Bill and Diane Wolff, and what fun we'd had with them in Taos and again at Thanksgiving in Desert Hot Springs. There were others, too many to list, some of whom I maintained contact with on Facebook, others through telephone calls and texts.

Now I'd found a network of kindred souls in Xscapers, all of us cloistered together in the desert as we sought safety from the Covid storm. I thought of Liza Simpson and Chris Wickland, a clothesline friendship that helped give me the strength to hang tough when I became discouraged.

But wait . . . What had happened to my commitment to travel light, to not drown myself with useless, worthless stuff that collected dust and distracted me from living?

Amazon happened, I'm embarrassed to admit. I'm committed to getting over this buying spree soon.

I enter the New Year with both fear for the future and joy in my heart. Although I remain frightened of Covid-19, rattlesnakes, and rats—and I should add Amazon to this list—I celebrate my happy, carefree life of nomadism. I rejoice to have found the Escapees, the Xscapers, and the RVillagers, all of whom helped me find community and helped us learn how to live on the road.

Had the coronavirus pandemic not struck, I might never have had the courage to sell my house, dispose of decades' worth of meaningless stuff, and take to the open road with no goal other than eking as much joy as possible from our remaining years. At this point, if either Michael or I should die from Covid-19, we'll exit knowing we ended in the most gloriously free lifestyle we've ever known.

How ironic that as the pandemic stripped us of so many freedoms, our RV lifestyle left us dizzy with the privilege of being on the road. I cringe to think we might have missed this journey.

On New Year's Eve, laundry had piled up. What the hell? I asked myself. It's not like I'm going to be kicking up my heels in celebration when they drop the Big Ball tonight in Times Square. I might as well do a load of laundry.

As I neared the laundry room, I pulled my mask over my mouth and nose.

At the entrance, I encountered an unmasked woman walking out the door towards a three-wheeled bicycle with a basket piled high with laundry.

"Oh, if it'll make you more comfortable," she said, "I'll put on a mask." She'd seen me pull on my mask.

I stopped, stunned. Finally, I said, "Yes, it'd make me much more comfortable. It might even save my life."

"You don't believe all this coronavirus hype, do you? she asked, pulling on a mask she'd retrieved from her basket. "This stuff is no worse than the seasonal flu, plus they're ruining the economy with all these shutdowns."

I stared at her, unable to respond.

She paid no attention to me as she grabbed her laundry basket and headed back inside.

I considered going back home, saving my dirty clothes for the afternoon or another day. Instead, I shrugged and went inside.

ABOUT THE AUTHOR

Gerri Almand began writing after forty years of social work practice. When her husband retired and proposed they buy an RV and travel the country, she reluctantly agreed. By the second year of bouncing down the road in their little tin-can house, Gerri began to realize RV travel was changing her in significant ways. Thus was born her first book—*The Reluctant RV Wife*. She hit a second homerun with her next release, *Home Is Where the RV Is*.

When Gerri and her husband left Tampa, Florida, in February 2020 on a two-month RV trip, they

had no way of predicting that a pandemic would erupt and leave them stranded in south Texas. Thus begins a terrifying yet glorious year of running for their lives. Realizing the RV offered protection and refuge, they sell their Florida home and transition to fulltime nomadism. Never looking back and regretting their decision, Gerri is stunned to realize that as governmental restrictions intensified during the pandemic, she and her husband discovered a freedom unlike anything they had ever previously known. She hopes her new story, *Running from Covid in our RV Cocoon*, will inspire readers to take risks and follow their dreams.

CPSIA information can be obtained
at www.ICGtesting.com
Printed in the USA
BVHW070710190621
609899BV00007B/1080